the
SPIRIT
ANIMAL
DIRECTORY
100 Spirit Animals for
INNER ENLIGHTENMENT

the
SPIRIT
ANIMAL
DIRECTORY

100 *Spirit Animals for*
INNER ENLIGHTENMENT

Dawn Baumann Brunke

chartwell
books

Brimming with creative inspiration, how-to projects, and useful information to enrich your everyday life, Quarto Knows is a favorite destination for those pursuing their interests and passions. Visit our site and dig deeper with our books into your area of interest: Quarto Creates, Quarto Cooks, Quarto Homes, Quarto Lives, Quarto Drives, Quarto Explores, Quarto Gifts, or Quarto Kids.

This edition published in 2021 by Chartwell Books,
an imprint of The Quarto Group
142 West 36th Street, 4th Floor
New York, NY 10018 USA
T (212) 779-4972 F (212) 779-6058
www.QuartoKnows.com

Originally published in 2015 as *The Key to Spirit Animals*.

Chartwell titles are also available at discount for retail, wholesale, promotional, and bulk purchase. For details, contact the Special Sales Manager by email at specialsales@quarto.com or by mail at The Quarto Group, Attn: Special Sales Manager, 100 Cummings Center Suite 265D, Beverly, MA 01915 USA

10 9 8 7 6 5 4

ISBN: 978-0-7858-3942-2

Library of Congress Control Number: 2020952593

Conceived, designed, and produced by
The Bright Press, an imprint of The Quarto Group.
The Old Brewery, 6 Blundell Street,
London N7 9BH, United Kingdom.
T (0)20 7700 6700
www.QuartoKnows.com

Design and layout by Clare Barber; Cover design by Emily Nazer
Illustrations by Joanna Kerr

Printed in China

This book provides general information. It should not be relied upon as recommending or promoting any specific diagnosis or method of treatment for a particular condition, and it is not intended as a substitute for medical advice or for direct diagnosis and treatment of a medical condition by a qualified physician. Readers who have questions about a particular condition, possible treatments for that condition, or possible reactions from the condition or its treatment should consult a physician or other.

MIX
Paper from
responsible sources
FSC® C016973

Grateful thanks to the many animal guides
who shared advice and helped me to write this
book, and to the many wise, supportive,
and inspiring spirit animals who help us all,
whether we are aware of it or not.

CONTENTS

INTRODUCTION

Throughout history, humans have been inspired by the speed, strength, intelligence, and beauty of animals. We are intrigued by their many unique abilities: to fly, to see in the dark, to breathe underwater, to camouflage themselves. Every animal species brings a distinct gift to our world—a special way of seeing things or a particular skill. Because there are many different animals on our planet, there are many diverse teachings. A soaring eagle brings us clarity of vision and a reminder to see larger perspectives. Spirit of Peacock encourages us to let our true colors shine or to reclaim inner beauty and express pride in who we are. Octopus recommends that we be flexible, curious, and adaptable.

THE SHAMANIC WAY

Shamanism is one of the world's oldest forms of spiritual practice. It is rooted in the experiential knowledge that we are not apart from, but an integral part of nature. As such, we are connected to all beings in a deeply profound way.

Ancient shamans knew the value of observing animals and studying their teachings. They formed personal relationships with power animals and journeyed with them through inner worlds. Spirit animals helped shamans to heal, advise, and solve problems.

A shaman woman connects with the spirit world.

They also served as protective companions through difficult situations.

Like modern-day shamans, we can learn to perceive teachings in nature and benefit from the experience and wisdom of animal guides. We too can discover our own spirit animals and develop ongoing relationships with them built upon trust and mutual respect.

INTRODUCTION

Deer is a skilled listener and gentle healer.

LIFE GUIDES

Some spirit animals work with us for a lifetime, helping us to develop our spiritual natures and achieve our soul's unique set of goals. Like master teachers, they follow our progress—cheering us on through our successes and helping us to learn from our mistakes. Sometimes we are aware of these guides; at other times they operate quietly in the background of our subconscious.

JOURNEYING COMPANIONS

Some spirit animals come to us for a short while to impart a specific teaching or assist in a particular situation. Alligator motivates us to be tough, persist through the task at hand, or arm ourselves with protection. Deer arrives to help us heal from trauma or learn to soften our heart through difficult times. Such animals may become journeying companions in our dreams and meditations, staying with us for as long as we need them.

MESSENGERS

Spirit animals may also act as messengers, delivering hints, clues, or inner nudges. Seeing a flock of geese flying in V-formation may remind us to streamline our pursuits, while the glimpse of a red fox inspires us to sharpen our senses or draw upon our clever, foxy nature. We may not form lasting relationships with such animals and their presence may be fleeting. Their assistance can be invaluable, however, in providing accurate, timely insights—if we are paying attention.

SHADOW GUIDES

Still other spirit animals challenge us. These are our shadow guides—the animals that help us to confront our fears or explore shadowy areas of our life that are stuck, stagnant, or in need of change and expansion. Such animals are often those we dislike or fear. And yet, these spirit animals may hold our most valuable teachings. For in learning to work with them, we begin to discover a truer version of who we really are.

THE PATH TO LEARNING

For the past 20 years I've been exploring, teaching, and writing about our deeper connections with animals. What I've learned is this: our ability to access animal wisdom and form meaningful partnerships with spirit animals depends a great deal upon our ability to open up in an authentic relationship with ourselves.

Associated with change and rebirth, Butterfly encourages us to be open to new experiences.

How do we that? I've found that the best learning is often achieved through experience. That's why the following pages are filled with meditations, dreaming and journaling exercises, and artistic projects that can assist you in getting to know yourself better. Think of the book as a buffet of tips, suggestions, and techniques—an invitation to try on different approaches in order to discover what works best for you.

The aim of this book is to engage spirit animals in more conscious ways. In Chapter One we'll use meditation and dreams to invoke creative encounters with animal guides. Chapter Two looks at ways to open awareness, deepen presence, and communicate with animals. In Chapter Three we'll fine-tune observational skills and learn to interpret the subtleties of what animal encounters mean.

Chapter Four offers a handy reference to the unique teachings of 96 animal guides. Brief descriptions of each animal's expertise are included along with questions, suggestions, and recommendations to benefit from their teachings. Lastly, Chapter Five explores practical ways to integrate our experiences as we develop deeper relationships with our spirit animals and with ourselves.

SEEK WITH AN OPEN HEART

The adventure ahead may require some effort and patience. You may become frustrated or hit a temporary dead end. My advice? Trust yourself. Trust the experience. Most animals sense and welcome our endeavors, especially when we convey a genuine desire for help.

Seek with an open heart and the natural world responds. Messages, answers, and clues arrive in wondrous ways, uniquely suited to our needs. A rainbow trout splashing in sunlit water, the cheerful trill of a robin's call, the moon-cast shadow of a lone coyote—all little smiles from the Universe reminding us that we're on the right track. Each sighting, sound, event, and encounter triggers a deeper form of knowing, a deeper connection not only with our spirit animals but with ourselves.

Animals can be incredibly wise and patient teachers. They are clever guides, insightful advisors, and thoughtful friends. What it takes from us is a willingness to be present, to perceive in deeper ways, and to open ourselves to heartfelt connection. Are you ready?

Spirit of Robin inspires creativity and alerts us to new opportunities.

KEYNOTE

The meditations in this book work best when spoken aloud. Consider recording them so you can play them back and listen as you meditate. Read slowly and calmly, allowing ample time for inner-world experiences. Ellipses in the meditation scripts indicate a brief pause. Bracketed notations indicate the suggested time for inner-world encounters. While recording, maintain silence (or, if you prefer, play soft music) for the duration of the time indicated. Each meditation can also be used as a template that you may individualize to your personal needs.

CHAPTER ONE

THE KEY TO
INNER-WORLD
EXPLORATION

○━► Explore interior pathways
through meditation

··

○━► Connect with the soul presence
of your lifelong animal guide

··

○━► Experience shamanic breathing
as a way to shift awareness

··

○━► Open gateways between
dreaming and waking states
of consciousness

THE JOURNEY

Exploring the inner world is a journey of shifting awareness. The adventure is usually marked by three stages: (1) leaving the framework of ordinary reality; (2) experiencing unusual encounters, dreamlike events, altered perceptions, and deep insights; and (3) returning to normal consciousness.

GOING WITHIN

Embarking upon the journey is a bit like entering a cave. We leave the bright familiarity of the everyday world and approach the dark unknown. It's shadowy in the cave, mysterious, and we don't know what's going to happen. Are there dangers ahead? Are we doing this right? Which way do we go?

Shhhhh . . . Breathe deeply. Release expectations and suppositions. Take a moment to savor the stillness.

OPENING TO A DIFFERENT PERCEPTION

As we relax, superficial mind chatter fades. As we let go of thinking, we begin to feel. Here, in quiet serenity, we open ourselves to another mode of perception.

As in dreams, inner-world imagery can be magical and wondrous. Perhaps you find yourself in a vivid landscape.

Journeys through interior landscapes may initially seem daunting. Trust yourself; welcome the adventure.

An animal approaches, offering to be your guide. As you journey together, you may be surprised by newfound abilities: to fly or move through walls. Your spirit animal whispers encouragement, reminding you of secrets you've always known.

We are able to journey in this way because we have awakened the right hemisphere of the brain—the intuitive part that perceives in empathic, imaginative, creative ways.

COMING OUT

Later, as the journey ends and we exit the cave, we might wonder: what was that about? We want to make sense of our inner-realm adventure, but in the bright light of the ordinary world those fascinating travels suddenly seem strange and enigmatic.

Luckily, we can draw upon the skills of our left brain—the organized, logical, interpretive side—to better comprehend our experiences. The left hemisphere notices detail and detects patterns. Its clear, precise manner can help us to anchor, translate, and decipher inner-world adventures within the framework of everyday life.

To fully embrace our encounters with spirit animals, it is helpful to be proficient as both sensitive explorer and sharp-eyed interpreter. We need to learn how to perceive and engage subtle dimensions, but we also need to understand the messages, clues, and guidance we receive.

BRIDGING WORLDS

The key to easy travel and translation between these states of consciousness lies in the center of our brain. Between the left and right hemispheres is a small bridge of connecting nerve fibers called the corpus callosum. Its job: to create a link and facilitate communication between the spheres.

Think of the corpus callosum as the sweet spot of the brain. It is a bridge, a pathway, between worlds. It allows us to access the unique strengths of both sides of our brain and integrate them in meaningful ways. Just as shamans travel easily between realms, we too can learn how to unite worlds by utilizing the whole of our brain. We too can learn to dance lightly in the in-between.

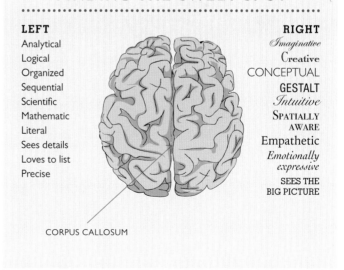

FINDING THE SWEET SPOT

LEFT
Analytical
Logical
Organized
Sequential
Scientific
Mathematic
Literal
Sees details
Loves to list
Precise

RIGHT
Imaginative
Creative
CONCEPTUAL
GESTALT
Intuitive
SPATIALLY
AWARE
Empathetic
*Emotionally
expressive*
SEES THE
BIG PICTURE

CORPUS CALLOSUM

MEDITATION: ONE MEANS TO TRAVEL DEEP

Slow your breathing, relax your mind, and awareness naturally deepens. In this simple and elegant way, meditation helps us to find our center, experience serenity, and access wisdom within. With practice, meditation is a means of transforming awareness. It also allows us to expand perspectives, journey through other realms, and interact with our spirit guides.

Much can be said about meditation but the best way to understand is through experience. The meditation on the opposite page makes use of a shamanic breathing technique to draw in grounding qualities from the Earth and expansive energies from the Sky. It is designed to help you find your center and use your breath as a vehicle for shifting awareness.

POST-MEDITATION

After completing the meditation, take time to record your experiences. What sensations did you have while breathing in from the Earth and Sky? Can you describe the experience of energies merging inside of you? What did it feel like as you exhaled through your center?

For maximum benefit, do this meditation several times. The awareness of how breathing can help you to ground, expand, and merge energy will be of great help as you later meet and journey with your animal guides. We will draw on this technique in other meditations.

♀ Meditation is a safe way to explore interior worlds.

SHAMANIC BREATHING MEDITATION

To begin, choose a quiet place where you won't be disturbed. Get comfortable—sitting, reclining—with part of your body in contact with the ground.

1. Close your eyes and take a few deep, easy breaths, in and out . . . As you relax, notice how your breathing shifts naturally between inhalation and exhalation . . .

2. Imagine now that you are breathing from the Earth, inhaling energy up from the ground. With each incoming breath, Earth energy moves into your feet, traveling up your legs and spine. Feel your connection with the Earth as you breathe its energy into your body. Feel it grounding you, stabilizing you, helping you to feel centered and secure . . .

3. Now imagine breathing from the top of your head. Just as you are connected to the Earth, you are connected to the Sky and Heavens. Take a moment to sense that connection, inhaling energy from the Sky. Feel it coming into your head, flowing downward through your neck and chest and arms . . .

4. And now, imagine you are breathing from both Earth and Sky simultaneously. It's a wonderful, curious feeling—the energies of Sky and Earth meeting inside of you, mingling and merging in the center of your being . . .

5. As you continue to breathe in an easy rhythm, imagine exhaling through the center of your chest and belly. It's an effortless process—inhaling from the Earth and Sky, and exhaling, easily, gently, through the center of your being.

6. Take a few moments here . . . Observe how simple breathing in and out connects the worlds above and below. Earth and Sky, inner and outer—all these energies mingling in the center of You. [1 to 2 minute pause for experience.]

7. When you are ready, gently guide your awareness back to your physical body . . . Take a few slow, deep breaths to refresh yourself as you return to normal consciousness.

THE IMPORTANCE OF JOURNALING

One easy and incredibly effective way to strengthen pathways between inner and outer worlds is to note down our experiences. Surprised? Consider this: the act of writing is a translation process. As we use our hands to write or type or draw, we physically tether our inner thoughts, ideas, and memories to physical reality. In this sense, a journal can literally bridge worlds!

A journal is also immensely practical. Memories of dream events and meditative encounters can quickly dissipate as we reengage in everyday activities. By journaling our experiences, we keep them safe. Journals provide a narrative record of our adventures that allows us to recall them in the future.

Some animal meetings or messages do not make immediate sense. We may be perplexed by clues we can't understand. A journal is a repository for all such mysteries and unanswered questions. That's why it's wise to take note of everything. Puzzling details may later be clarified or provide a key to unlocking larger teachings.

Journaling about our adventures with spirit animals also helps to establish good working relationships. It reveals our desire to connect with them and our willingness to put forth efforts to learn. It confirms that such experiences are important to us.

Lastly, journals can provide excellent reference material for future exploration. We can use journal entries to follow up on teachings, review advice, or launch dialogues to further explore areas of interest with our animal guides.

The bottom line: To anchor recall and provide a reliable record of all your spirit animal adventures, a journal is invaluable.

A journal is essential for the serious inner-world adventurer.

CREATE A SPIRIT ANIMAL JOURNAL

Create a master journal to record everything—meditative experiences, dreams, animal encounters—or separate journals for each activity. Use a fabric-bound book, inexpensive notebook or three-ring binder. No matter how you organize it, you'll benefit greatly.

NOTE IT—Record everything! What happened? Which animals appeared? What were their actions? What about their demeanor? Note your feelings, thoughts, and questions—as well as anything puzzling, unusual, or nonsensical—for further exploration.

DRAW IT—Sketch animal expressions, postures, or gestures for quicker recall. Draw a map if traveling was involved or to indicate position or movement of characters within a scene. Sometimes a picture truly is worth a thousand words.

DATE IT—Include the year, month, day, hour, and minute. Time notation can sometimes provide a valuable clue, especially when exploring larger patterns and ongoing themes.

TITLE IT—Titles offer quick reference and stimulate recall. Choose distinct, intriguing headings that will prompt your memory. (Examples from my journal: "Two Snakes in a Cold Car," "The Golden Butterflies," "Dancing with the Polar Bear.")

SUPPLEMENT IT—If desired, include research about the animals you encounter. For example, you might note their physical attributes, habits in nature, or totemic qualities and teachings.

SUMMARIZE IT—Though not essential, a one-sentence summary can help to spur your memory and is a good exercise in identifying key points.

MEET YOUR LIFELONG ANIMAL GUIDE

You may interact with a wide variety of spirit animals during your lifetime. Some may stay with you for a while, while others are short-term visitors. You also have a lifelong guide, a protective spirit animal that has been with you since the beginning.

Many times we already have a sense of this guide—maybe you have an ongoing passion for lions or dogs; maybe you are continually drawn to elephants or whales. For some, such spirit guides are present in daily life and we are already conscious of them. For others, spirit animals live in the background of the psyche. Perhaps we're not aware of their presence or teaching except in a subconscious way.

The following meditation is designed to help you meet your lifelong animal guide. As you invite your spirit animal to be present, the meditation may spur childhood memories of a beloved pet, stuffed animal toy, or imaginary animal friend. Then again, you may be very surprised by the animal that shows up.

The meditation will help you to connect with the heart-and-soul presence of your animal. The aim is to open a gateway so that you can initiate contact with your spirit animal and create a healthy foundation for a relationship. Following the meditation, use the Journal Prompts to write about your experience.

Animal guides may appear soft and cuddly in early childhood.

ANIMAL GUIDE MEDITATION

As with the last meditation, choose a quiet spot where you won't be disturbed.
Settle into a comfortable position sitting or lying on the ground.

1. Close your eyes and take a few deep, easy breaths, in and out . . .

2. Feel the solid stability of the Earth beneath you. Imagine that you are breathing upward from the Earth. Feel its energy connecting with you, helping to ground and support you, helping you to feel at home on planet Earth . . .

3. Just as you are connected to the Earth, you are connected to the Sky and Universe. Take a moment to acknowledge that connection . . . Feel Sky energy flowing into the top of your head, moving through your body . . .

4. As you breathe up from the Earth and down from the Sky—easily, naturally—begin to feel those energies mingling inside of you. Notice how they join together in the center of your being . . . Feel yourself deepening, relaxing, enjoying your calm, quiet center.

5. Next, we'll travel inward. Allow your breath to gently guide you as you sink deeper within. Down, down, down your awareness flows, to a place that seems to call you. Perhaps it is a meadow or a river, a mountain or a lake.

6. Relax. You do not have to visualize anything. All that you need will reveal itself to you. Feel the ground beneath you, the air upon your face. Make yourself at home. Look . . . Listen . . . Feel . . . Allow yourself to be fully present.

7. Breathing in and out, feeling very comfortable in this safe, relaxing space, invite your spirit animal to be present with you now. Open your heart and mind, and sincerely welcome your spirit animal—the one who has been with you all along, helping you, supporting you, protecting you . . .

8. Some animals are bold. Some are playful and comical. Others are shy and reserved. Be open to whatever form or shape your animal uses to appear to you. It may be different than the way the animal appears in waking life.

9. Take several minutes to watch and listen. Allow this unique first encounter to unfold in its own way, in its own time. [Allow 2 minutes for experience.]

10. Still very relaxed within yourself, ask your spirit animal if it has a message for you. It may be conveyed as a visual symbol, a thought, or a feeling—a gesture, an idea, or a sound. Look . . . Listen . . . [30 seconds for experience.]

JOURNAL PROMPTS

*How did your spirit animal reveal itself?
Describe its size, shape, color, and demeanor.
How did it move? What actions did it take?
Did it have a message for you? What were
your feelings—surprise? Excitement?
Hesitation? Disappointment?*

*Your journal is just for you, so be honest in
recording all emotional aspects of your
experience. If something feels puzzling or
scary, write about it. As you continue to work
with your spirit animals, you may notice
changes in your thoughts and feelings. Come
back to your journal to note those too.*

11. Even if it seems as if nothing is happening, trust this experience. Trust this invitation for deeper connection. Perhaps your animal will come to you later, in a dream or daydream.

12. Whatever your experience, allow all of the sensations and details to fill your being, knowing that you will remember all you need to know. Take another minute to experience this connection, to simply be present with your spirit animal. [1.5 minutes for experience.]

13. And now it's time to thank your animal, to say goodbye, and ready yourself to leave. Know that you can return to this shared space of connection whenever you choose . . .

14. When you feel that you are ready, use your breath to travel up, up, up—back toward conscious awareness . . .

15. Feel yourself grounded within your body, supported by the Earth, guided by the Sky. Open your eyes, awake, aware, refreshed.

KEYNOTE

If you want to deepen your connection with your animal and learn more, consider placing a figurine or photo of your guide in a place where you'll see it daily. We can strengthen our relationships with spirit animals by keeping them present in our mind. You may want to add flowers, feathers, crystals, or a special stone (or whatever speaks to you) as a way to honor the experience. Look to Chapter Two for additional ways to engage spirit animal teachings in everyday life.

DREAMING

I once dreamed of a small orange cat that wore an ornate hat with a feather tassel. The cat sat on a table and looked at me with watchful composure. On waking I drew a sketch of the enigmatic cat and wondered why she had visited my dreams.

Many years later, I dreamed again of the mysterious cat with the fancy hat. She came several more times, always observing me silently, as if waiting for something. I was intrigued by the cat. I wanted to connect with her and understand why she kept visiting my dreams. I drew images of her in my journal and pondered the significance of her posture, attitude, and possible teaching. When I finally realized the cat was one of my spirit animals, she rewarded me by telling me her secret name. Thus our relationship deepened and our adventures began.

FIRST CONTACT

Many animal guides prefer to initiate contact in the dream world. Perhaps it's because we are less judgmental there, less rigidly insistent about what can and cannot be true. We can more easily accept the idea of a talking cat or be more willing to listen to the advice of a coyote in our dreams than in waking life. Dream consciousness opens us to creative possibilities.

Like my orange cat, some animal guides appear in our dreams to observe and test our readiness for their teachings. Pay attention and you may be rewarded. The dream world is a richly inventive realm that allows us to interact with our animal guides in innumerable ways. The first challenge, however, is to remember the dream!

Intuitive and observant, Cat nudges us toward deeper self-discovery.

TIPS FOR DREAM RECALL

WELCOME IT—Linger in the borderland that links dreams with waking consciousness. Keep the pathway open by inviting your dreams to remain present in your awareness on awakening. Review dream scenarios and images before opening your eyes.

SPEAK IT—Say your dream aloud before rising from bed. This is a very effective way to hold dreams for later recall.

NOTE IT—Record dreams as soon as possible. Keep your journal handy. Most dreams evaporate easily. Making a habit of dream notation will help you to strengthen both retention and recall.

NOTICE IT—No matter how strange, subtle, or insignificant they seem, tiny details often yield great treasure. Some spirit animals first show up in symbolic ways—a feather, a paw print, a distant call. Be aware and alert to everything as you review your dream and record it.

TRUST IT—Even if all you can recall is the fragment of an image or the whisper of a feeling, write it down. Some dreams require a bit of attention before they unfold.

RESPECT IT—The level of respect we show our dreams—and dream animals—reveals our readiness for their teaching. Cultivate a sincere approach to learning more. Your guides will notice.

MEETING SPIRIT ANIMALS IN THE DREAM WORLD

We don't know what stories our dreams will share. Part of their mystery and allure is that they simply happen. We close our eyes, nod off, and suddenly find ourselves immersed in vivid dramas that seem so real we don't think to question their validity.

Because the rules of reality are more fluid and open in the dream world, many spirit animals choose to interact with us there. For humans, it's a safe place to meet some of these powerful beings and explore different perspectives of reality. In our dreams we can soar on thermal winds with Raven, plunge off an iceberg with Penguin, or stalk the dark jungle with Tiger.

Some animals show up to inspire and challenge us through dream journeys. They may invite us to fly, swim, or run as fast as they do. By engaging us in dream activities, spirit animals can awaken skills and strengths we never knew we had. They may offer answers to questions we haven't yet asked or share their unique viewpoints, helping us to see things in completely different ways.

So, how do we encourage such dreams? To show your readiness for a dream-world encounter with your animal guide, consider invoking a meeting.

Dream-world travel opens us to new vistas and expansive realms of awareness.

INVOKE A DREAM MEETING

PAVE THE WAY—Before going to bed, announce your desire for a dream encounter. Do this in a way that is meaningful for you. For example, place a favorite gemstone or crystal under your pillow to enhance dream-world travel and clarity of awareness. Create a dream altar by placing several animal photos or figurines on your nightstand. Choose animals that you feel drawn to or that you sense may help you with your pursuit. Keep your journal nearby as a sign that you intend to write about your dreams. It's not so much what you do, but the intention with which you do it. Be artistic and witty, or solemn and ceremonious—what matters is that you express your true feelings and treat the process with care. Pave the way for deeper, more meaningful encounters by showing interest and respect.

REQUEST ASSISTANCE—Before falling asleep, request assistance. Be clear about what you want—is it to meet a particular animal? To get help on a specific problem? To explore the wonders of the dream world with a personal guide? Speak your desire aloud or meditate on it for a few moments. Write a note to your animal guide, send a mental invitation to the dream world, or appeal to the community of spirit animals for support. The more focused and genuine the approach, the greater chances for being heard—and helped.

END WITH THANKS—On waking, thank your spirit animals for all their help. Even if no animals appeared, give thanks for any assistance behind the scenes. Your animal may appear another night or perhaps during waking hours. Respect your spirit animal guides, and they will respond in kind.

WAKING IN YOUR DREAM, DREAMING WHILE AWAKE

For additional fun in exploring the connections between inner and outer worlds, take a twofold approach: dream while waking, wake while dreaming. What does that mean? It means finding ways to bring dream elements into your waking life, and waking elements into your dreams, whether that is through lucid dreaming or by entering the dream world through daydreams.

Let's think of dreaming as a three-stage process. We first fall asleep and enter the dream cave, or inner theater of the mind. Our dreams occur in the second stage. There, events and encounters take place in a special state of consciousness, apart from the ordinary world. Stage three involves waking up, recalling our dreams, and (hopefully) acting upon them in some way, thus bringing the process full circle.

The boundary between waking and dreaming is not geographic; rather, it's a shift in consciousness. When we dream we tune in to a different vibration, a different frequency of awareness. You are still you when you are dreaming—and yet, you are somewhere else.

LUCID DREAMING

Lucid dreaming is a special form of dreaming, in which we become aware that we are in a dream. It's an unusual and often thrilling in-between place of knowing in which we simultaneously have access to two states of consciousness—waking and dreaming. Lucid dreams allow us to travel unique trails that blend our dreams with waking life. Though such dreaming generally happens unexpectedly, we can also learn to invoke lucid dreams.

Dreamscapes may appear strange, unusual, and otherworldly.

♀ Skilled in moving through
inner worlds, Seal is a helpful
guide to lucid dreaming.

One method is to repeat a favorite phrase or look for a specific object that is already anchored in waking life. For example, before going to sleep tell yourself that when you look at your hands in your dream, you will remember that you are dreaming. This may require some time and patience, but it can be very effective.

You can also ask your spirit animal guides to help you initiate a lucid dream. Some animals specialize in dreaming. A few that are experts in lucid-dream states include Bear (especially Polar Bear), Seal, and Lizard.

JOINING WORLDS

Joining dream consciousness with waking awareness is not only fun but enlightening. Some animal guides are particularly good at leaving clues or messages in both worlds concurrently. It can become a game to find hints, discover associations, uncover correspondences, and witness the larger, more meaningful connections that emerge. Play the game and you may expand yourself in ways unforeseen.

A few suggestions on how to begin: practice entering the dream world by daydreaming or cultivating very relaxed states of awareness. Use meditative journeys as a stepping-stone to reenter your dreams. Once there, explore the dreamscape anew. Slip into waking dreams by utilizing your imagination. Engage your dream animals in conversation. Ask how they travel between worlds. Listen to their advice and brainstorm ways that you might do the same.

KEYNOTE

Be resourceful, innovative, and experimental. Welcome and consider all wild ideas. Embracing creativity is an excellent way to open ourselves to multiple perspectives and thus appreciate our experiences even more.

CHAPTER TWO

THE KEY TO
RELATIONSHIPS
AND
COMMUNICATION

 Expand your awareness to
perceive beyond the physical

....

 Learn to recognize animal
messengers when they arrive

....

 Discover creative, practical
ways to engage animal teachings
in everyday life

....

 Participate in the Universal
Language by having a talk with
your spirit animal

ESTABLISH A CONNECTION WITH THE NATURAL WORLD

The ways in which we connect with nature and animals are foundational to our relationship with them. Do we notice the animals that appear and offer guidance? Do we pay attention to how the natural world supports us? By being attentive to what is happening around us, we may be surprised to discover that meaning and assistance is everywhere.

Many years ago, while attending a spiritual retreat, I awoke early in the morning and stepped outside my cabin to greet the sunrise. The past days had been confusing and filled with self-doubt, but as the first rays of sunshine met my face, everything became brilliantly clear. The sudden sensation of golden light filling my body was so profound that I felt a physical jolt.

"Is this real?" I wondered. Just then, a large gray dog called Smokey bounded up the porch. Guardian of the retreat grounds, he ran to me and nudged his soft muzzle into my hand. Stepping back, he met my gaze, wagged his tail and barked three times. Then he was off, leaving just as quickly as he had arrived.

The natural world speaks to us without ever uttering a word.

The experience lasted less than a minute, yet it changed everything. Though the rush of sunshine had graced me with clarity, old habits of doubt surfaced all too quickly. I was then graced a second time. The timely arrival of a trustworthy and openhearted animal messenger offered physical reassurance (a warm muzzle) and an unmistakable answer (a look, a wag, and three loud barks) to my question: Yes, this is real!

ANIMAL MESSENGERS

Animal messengers may visit us in astonishing and remarkable ways. They have an uncanny knack of showing up just when we need them. Like Smokey the dog, they arrive at key junctures or pivotal moments in our life. They seem to know exactly what we need: encouragement, advice, inspiration, or simple reassurance that all is well. And then—they are gone.

To both welcome and recognize your animal messengers, it's wise to pay attention—not only while doing meditations and dream work, but all the time. The world is filled with hints and clues; nature is continually speaking to us.

Dog cheers us on with love and encouragement.

The following meditations are about establishing a connection with the natural world and learning to perceive in deeper ways so that you'll better recognize your animal teachers when they appear.

I recommend that you try both meditations several times. Choose different animals and locations for variety. Take your time with these meditations. They may seem simple, but they are powerful.

SOFT-EYES NATURE MEDITATION

This meditation invokes a soft, dreamy, intuitive way of perceiving energy. By relaxing your vision and using "soft eyes," you may begin to sense beneath fur and feathers, and appreciate the deeper presence of an animal. Find a quiet place outdoors near an animal that is likely to stay present for a time—a duck in a lake or a cow in a pasture. You can also do this with your dog or cat at home.

3. Now you notice the way your animal is breathing, or the way it moves. Let your vision go blurry or unfocused if it wants. Let the image of your animal wash over you . . .

4. Now imagine your vision relaxing into your animal. Open yourself to the deeper sense of presence that emanates from its being . . .

1. Close your eyes and use the shamanic breathing technique (pages 16–17) to connect with Earth and Sky. Take several minutes to center. [Allow 2 minutes.]

5. Take some time to experience and enjoy. [Allow a minimum of 5 minutes.]

2. Breathing easily, slowly open your eyes and look toward your animal. Let your vision settle on it in a soft, gentle way . . .

6. When you are finished, take a moment to thank your animal. Blink your eyes several times and use your breath to return to normal consciousness.

JOURNAL PROMPTS

What happened? Were you surprised that simply relaxing your vision allowed you to perceive in a different way? What did you discover about your animal? Did you have any difficulties? If so, what can you change as you try this meditation again?

WALKING IN NATURE MEDITATION

Using movement to deepen and center is an ancient form of meditation. The rhythmic motion of walking is calming and induces a natural meditative state. This activity involves walking for about 30 minutes, so listening to a recorded meditation may not be practical. Instead, familiarize yourself with the instructions before beginning. It's best to do this meditation in a quiet, uncrowded park, garden, nature trail, or field.

1. Stand still and take a few deep breaths. Give each part of your body—feet, limbs, torso, neck, and head—a little attention, encouraging relaxation.

2. Begin walking at a normal pace. Notice the way your feet touch the earth as they alternate with each step. Let yourself enjoy this soothing, natural rhythm.

3. As you ease into this tranquil flow, allow your senses to do the same. Use "soft eyes" and "soft ears" to perceive your surroundings. You may become aware of the grass in a different way. Perhaps there are animals nearby. You may not see them, but you might feel their presence.

4. You may notice that your senses are heightened or your consciousness has expanded beyond the confines of your body. You may feel attuned to, and a part of, the larger flow of nature.

5. Enjoy the rhythm of your body's movement, the calming of your mind, and the deepening of awareness.

6. When you feel your meditation is at a natural close, take a few deep breaths to return to normal consciousness.

7. Take a few moments to sit or rest before journaling. At first, it may seem as if nothing has happened. Remember, this meditation is not about outward experience; it's about what is happening within.

JOURNAL PROMPTS

Are you surprised by how different you feel after this meditation? Rather than describing your experiences in the usual way, you may want to try something new. Consider a poetic style of journaling and jot down key images, colors, sounds, feelings, and sensations with single words or phrases. Honor your meditative experience by expressing yourself in the way that feels best to you.

COMMUNICATE WITH ANIMALS

Communing with the natural world and conversing with animals is nothing new. Our ancestors did it. They were able to understand and communicate with a wide variety of animals—wolves, geese, ants, and whales—by tuning in to a common language that was shared by all. This Universal Language was not based on words or honks or howls, but feeling.

Children talk to animals naturally, without fear or judgment.

Communicating with animals is part of being human. Though it's a skill our modern culture has mostly set aside, the ability is within us all. With a little effort and an open mind, you too can begin to recall the Universal Language of all life.

THE UNIVERSAL LANGUAGE

Because most animals do not speak English, conversation with them requires us to utilize a shared language. Animal communication is an intuitive process. By engaging the right side of our brain we can tune into the impressions, thoughts, and feelings of other animals.

To make sense of what the right side of the brain receives, the left side of the brain translates. It decodes the feelings, sensations, and impressions we have when communing with an animal in ways that make sense to us. Think of it as engaging a universal translator device that allows us to understand the thoughts of other species through the software of our brain.

HOW DOES IT WORK?

The way in which we receive communications from an animal depends to some degree on how we perceive in the world. For example, if you are very visual, you may see images or inner movies that depict what an animal is attempting to convey. If you are empathic, you may sense emotions. Some people hear thoughts, as if listening to an inner conversation.

In a similar way, we can use mental images (see it), feelings (sense it), or thoughts (mentally say it) to convey our ideas to animals. Don't worry about which way is best. When you are in the flow of connection, it will happen.

THREE STEPS TO TALKING WITH ANIMALS

1. CENTER, CONNECT, ATTUNE—Step one is to calm, center, and deepen in consciousness. From that space we can more easily connect with an animal's presence. Attuning means tuning in to an animal's frequency—similar to tuning the dial on a radio to find a particular station. Connecting and attuning allows us to move deeper into a relationship and initiate conversation.

2. LOOK, LISTEN, PERCEIVE—Step two is opening ourselves to hear, see, perceive, and experience. Be patient, relaxed, receptive. Welcome what comes. Answers may arrive via image, thought, sensation, word, smell, taste, or even a gestalt of knowing. Don't judge—allow the experience to unfold.

3. SAY GOODBYE, END WITH THANKS—The last step is to close your connection. Saying goodbye helps to clear the energy between you and your animal. By offering thanks, you acknowledge your appreciation and create a good foundation for future talks.

The meditation on the following pages will help you to initiate a talk with your spirit animal. For a first attempt, you might choose your lifelong guide from Chapter One. Once you feel comfortable talking with your spirit animal, try the meditation with other animal guides or physical animals at home.

With deepened presence, we may easily recall the Universal Language of all life.

A TALK WITH YOUR SPIRIT ANIMAL

1. Spend several minutes using your breath to relax and center. [Allow a minimum of 3 minutes.]

2. As you deepen, invite the self that has always known how to converse with animals to be present in your consciousness. This part of you is comfortable opening the heart and mind to deep communion with your animal.

3. From that space of deepened connection and presence, invite your spirit animal to be present with you now . . .

4. Perhaps you see your animal in your mind's eye. Or perhaps you sense its presence near you. Simply be open and welcome its arrival. [1 minute.]

5. As you become more aware of your animal's presence, gently guide your consciousness to expand outward. Imagine a bridge of light connecting you and your animal. This bridge will allow you to communicate in a safe, comfortable, and clear manner. [30 seconds.]

6. When you are ready, offer greetings to your spirit animal. Let it know why you've requested this talk. You can use thoughts or feelings or images. Speak from your heart and express what you most need or want to say. Take a moment now to share with your animal. [1 minute.]

7. And now, ask your animal to share whatever it would most like you to know. Your animal's message may be a sound or an image, a thought or a feeling. Listen deeply without judging what you perceive. [1 minute.]

8. And now, before finishing this brief conversation, ask your animal for a symbol that represents its key teaching to you. You may hear a phrase or see a mental picture. Perhaps you recall a memory, or sense an emotion such as excitement or well-being. Take a moment to be open to whatever comes. [1 minute.]

9. Trust this experience, even if it seems as if nothing has happened. Your spirit animal may come to you later. Simply by being present in this space, you are opening connections . . .

10. Thank your animal for connecting with you. And thank yourself for being open. Know that you can return to this shared space of connection whenever you choose.

11. Say goodbye to your animal and use your breath to return to center. When you feel grounded within your body, open your eyes to waking consciousness.

JOURNAL PROMPTS

Record your experiences with special attention to your spirit animal's message and symbol. How did you feel in relation to your animal? Friendly? Distant? Some spirit animals are direct and no-nonsense, while others may be easygoing and affable. Your relationship with your spirit animal may change over time. It can be useful—and quite revealing—to note your feelings at early stages and later compare them, as your relationship evolves.

It can be surprising to suddenly discover a spirit animal that has been protecting and guiding us for a very long time.

BUILD BRIDGES

Small gatherings of ceramic, stone, metal, and wood figurines sit atop my desk and dresser, window ledge, and nightstand. Dog, Bear, Giraffe, Hippo—they come from all over the world, bought in foreign countries, crafted by local artists, found in thrift stores, given to me by friends. Each one speaks in its own way, some reminding me to be strong or focused, others encouraging me to carry on.

There are many inventive ways that we can evoke the teachings of our spirit animals and elicit their assistance in everyday life. For example, if I feel a need to get hopping with a project, I might place my little wood carving of Frog in front of my computer. If I need to be discerning and insightful, a small pewter statue of Cat may accompany me that day.

As you learn more about the teachings of various animals, you may want to collect small figurines or carvings that hold special significance for you. Then, when you need a particular animal's help, invite one to ride in your pocket or purse, or to sit on your desk for the day. There are many other creative and practical ways to both call upon and honor a spirit animal's teaching. Here are just a few.

Hand-carved figurines may evoke an animal's presence.

Personalizing an animal altar can be artistic, inspired, and fun.

CONSULT AN ORACLE

Consciously choosing to engage the teaching of a certain animal can be helpful in aligning you with its assistance, but what if you're not sure which animal to choose? Or what if you don't know about the teachings of any animals? In such cases, you might benefit from using animal oracle cards.

Oracle cards are a fun and simple way to explore animal teachings and receive the guidance you need. You can buy a deck of animal cards or create your own by adhering animal photos or images onto cards. Shuffle the deck facedown as you think about what you need help with or most want to know. Then, use your intuition to choose a card.

Turn it over and take a moment to feel this animal's presence. Pay attention to your inner knowing before reading what others say about the animal's teaching. In this way, you encourage yourself to consult your own feelings first. Later, when researching your animal's teaching, you may discover that you know more than you think you do!

ARRANGE AN ALTAR

Arrange small statues, photos, or artwork of your animal on a shelf, table, or ledge in your home. Or, make several altars—in your office, garden, bedroom, and kitchen—so that you see them at different times.

Altars allow us to get creative and tap into deeper connections. They also provide daily reminders of our alliance with an animal. Add flowers, crystals, stones, or objects found in nature that speak to you about your animal. In some countries, small amounts of food are offered to altar animals in supplication.

If you are working with several animal guides, why not include them all? An altar that combines animals can amplify individual teachings and blend group energies in interesting ways.

The author's polar bear necklace—scrimshaw on fossilized ivory.

CARRY A FETISH

A fetish is a small representation of an animal (usually stone, wood, or bone) that carries its teaching. Similar to an amulet or talisman, a fetish may bring protection or luck, but it is also considered by some to be imbued with the spirit of the animal. Carrying a fetish allows one to draw upon that animal's power and expertise.

You can create your own fetish by making or buying a small animal figure and energetically infusing it in ways that are meaningful to you. For example, you might bless it, meditate or dream with it, or personalize it with small charms. A fetish not only serves to remind us of our connection with a spirit animal, but it may also inspire us to connect in deeper ways with all life.

WEAR A SYMBOL

Another way to carry an animal's teaching with you is to wear it! While working on a book about polar bears, I acquired a scrimshaw necklace carved with the image of a mother polar bear protecting her baby in an icy Arctic setting. Wearing it reminded me both of the heartiness and strength of polar bears, and of their gentle guidance.

Consider wearing rings, bracelets, or pendants that feature your animal's likeness. Some spirit animals may encourage us to do just that. I once had a powerful dream about an alligator and the very next day found a tiny rhinestoned alligator pendant while shopping for something else. Be alert to such hints and inspired nudges from your animal guides.

Use feathers to invite bird wisdom and Sky energy.

CELEBRATE ART

Paint, draw, sketch, sculpt, or mold portrayals of your spirit animal. Or, purchase artwork featuring your animal and display it somewhere you will see it daily.

If you like performance art, consider making sounds or movements that invoke the spirit of your animal. For example, play with moving like a bear or howling like a coyote to awaken the powers of those animal spirits within yourself.

The more ways you find to activate energetic connections with your animal guides, the stronger the link and clearer the pathway between you.

CREATE FROM NATURE

Engage your artistic self by creating your own clothes, jewelry, or accessories that incorporate physical aspects of your animal—such as claws, fur, or feathers. A friend of mine who was working with Crow spent time each day watching the crows that visited her backyard. She later collected some of their dropped feathers and bound them together with thread. She added beads, a thin wash of gold paint and a fastener to create a unique, beautiful, and personally meaningful headpiece that honored her connection with Crow.

Artwork may evoke emotional qualities of an animal's teaching.

43

NOTICE EVERYTHING

Some would say that spirit animals are all around us all the time. In this light, the quest to align ourselves with an animal teacher isn't so much about how to find it, as how to notice its presence.

By encouraging a playful sense of curiosity and open awareness, you may find clues and messages from animal messengers shining through the most ordinary of activities—shopping at a grocery store, chatting with a friend, or sitting at home watching television.

Intelligent, inquisitive, and sometimes humorous, Bear is both an engaging and powerful teacher.

HELLO BEAR!

For example, let's say Bear wants your attention. It may first call to you in a passing way—a bear tattoo you notice on a stranger's arm. You later notice the beautiful silver pendant your friend is wearing, designed in the shape of a bear paw. That evening, you find yourself gazing at a larger-than-life painting of a bear's face that hangs in a fancy restaurant—which just happens to be named Orso, meaning "bear" in Italian.

Do you see how it happens? From all the myriad events and encounters that occur, Bear summons your attention through a series of subtle (and some not-so-subtle) clues. A physical bear need not be present. Rather, the spirit of Bear calls to you through the bright colors of a tattoo, the stylized shape of its paw, a close-up of its face, and a physical location that bears its name.

While opening yourself to animal teachings, be alert to repeating themes and patterns, intriguing images, unusual meetings, or synchronous happenings. Take time to engage all of your senses and notice the symbolic hints that come your way.

A LESSON IN TRUST

The ways in which spirit animals interact with us are often amazingly clever and exceedingly appropriate. The following meditation is an exercise in letting go and trusting that the animal messenger who responds is the one best suited to address our needs.

Before beginning the meditation, think of a question that has meaning and importance for you. Maybe you need insight on a relationship or upcoming decision. Perhaps you feel stuck and don't know why. Hone in on what you really want to know. Be succinct. Generally speaking, the more specific the request, the more specific the answer.

Animal guides may show up in unexpected places, in unexpected ways.

Whenever we request help from spirit animals with genuine desire, we receive an answer. While it may not be the answer we want or hope to have, it will be the answer we need—the one that will help us most.

You may be surprised, shocked, or amused at the animal that responds to your request. Your guide may appear as a real animal or as an image in a book, movie, or painting. Perhaps it comes to you in a daydream, sudden thought, or memory. It may come as an animal call or as tracks you see on the ground.

INVOKING ANIMAL GUIDANCE

1. Find a quiet, comfortable place and spend a few moments centering. As you deepen, make contact with the part of yourself that genuinely needs help or guidance.

2. When you are ready, focus on your question. Feel the significance of your request and state it aloud or silently in your mind . . .

3. Now, ask for a sign or encounter from the animal world—something that will help you understand what you most need to know . . .

4. And now, let it go! Imagine your question floating like a balloon into the sky, carried away by a gentle wind. You are releasing your concern into a larger space, a more expansive realm . . .

5. As you return to conscious awareness, know that the answer to your question will come when the time is right. The only job you have is to be present for the animal that appears. Trust that you will recognize your answer when it arrives.

6. Pay attention to animals that show up in the next few days. Allow your consciousness to be relaxed and open. You are not so much looking for something as simply being aware, calmly attentive to the events that unfold. You may forget about your question and then suddenly—an animal appears, and you know you have your answer.

JOURNAL PROMPTS

*Of course you'll want to describe your animal, its actions, and the circumstances
that accompanied its appearance. But add other significant details too:
Where did the event happen? What were you doing or thinking when it occurred?
Did you receive a clear message or do you have more to consider?
You may want to learn more about your animal, or honor its teaching in some way.
Perhaps this animal will continue to help you in the future.*

STAY OPEN

Welcome and accept opportunities to work with a variety of teachers. Try new things to experience different perspectives. Be spontaneous and flexible. Listen to what calls you.

Use meditations, dreams, walks in nature, and conversations with animals to build a strong foundation of connection. The more you exercise your intuition, the more sensitive you become.

Expand your awareness to perceive beyond the physical. By sensing deep, you deepen yourself; deepen yourself and you deepen your connections with the world.

Messages from the natural world are all around us. Take time to look, listen, and feel.

THREE TIPS TO DEEPEN YOUR RELATIONSHIP WITH YOUR ANIMAL GUIDE

1. **BE PRESENT**—Forget texting and multitasking. If you want to cultivate a strong and meaningful relationship with an animal teacher, be fully present and accountable. Give all your attention to every encounter and experience.

2. **BE AUTHENTIC**—Humans sometimes say one thing and mean another. It's confusing to animals and in the end confusing to ourselves. Be clear about what you feel and express it plainly. Are you nervous, frightened, apprehensive? By acknowledging your true feelings, you establish authenticity in yourself and in your dealings with others.

3. **BE A GOOD PARTNER**—Deep relationships with spirit animals require mutual trust and respect. Be honest and sensitive as you hold up your end of the conversation. Sometimes animal guides need our support too. Learn to give as well as receive.

CHAPTER THREE

THE KEY TO

CLEAR
INTERPRETATION

○—➤ Strengthen intuition
and build confidence through
real-world experience

○—➤ Journal with your shadow
animal to learn more about who
you really are

○—➤ Learn to identify patterns, uncover
themes, and discover hidden clues

○—➤ Celebrate interpretation
as a form of art

IS IT REAL?

One of the first obstacles you may encounter while working with animal teachers—particularly in beginning stages—is the wall of skepticism. You receive a brilliant insight from an animal but are soon dashed by doubts. Is this real? you wonder. Maybe I'm making this up. Maybe I'm just imagining it all.

If this happens to you, step back and take a deep breath. Remind yourself that reality checks are valuable. At times it is appropriate to be skeptical. Without a healthy dose of skepticism we might lose ourselves in wishful thinking or projecting our own desires and dreams onto animals.

So, how do we know if we are interpreting an animal message correctly, in a way that is relevant to our situation? The best answer I have found: experience. Seek confirmation in the real world. Put your intuition to the test. Empower yourself with proof. For example, perhaps you intuit something from your neighbor's dog that you couldn't possibly have known otherwise, but is later verified for you by your neighbor. Or, maybe you act upon advice that an animal gives you, and later see how it was both timely and beneficial.

As we seek and receive confirmations more consistently, we build confidence. We notice when we are perceiving clearly and when we are not. We can feel what resonates strongly and what feels forced or fuzzy. With practice and experience, we can know when our interpretations are on target and when they miss the mark.

⚲ Trust intuitive feelings and seek verification from others.

TIPS TO FINE-TUNE YOUR FEELINGS

TAKE A BREAK—If feeling stuck, confused, or overwhelmed, take a break. Have a bath, take a walk, sit in nature, or go on a drive. Sometimes we need to get away in order to regain our center and readjust our views.

ACKNOWLEDGE AND ACCEPT—It's best to acknowledge feelings of uncertainty up front. Accept your doubts and investigate them. How we deal with our feelings is part of the learning process. By being honest with yourself, you open pathways for clearer perceptions and better understanding.

BE A DETECTIVE—Interpretation may require us to follow clues. Some things don't make sense in the moment, but will later on. A puzzling animal encounter may hold signs that lead to additional events in which deeper understanding unfolds. Take note of hints and follow inner nudges for further investigation.

CONSIDER OTHER PERSPECTIVES—If you are feeling close but not quite on target with an interpretation, try sensing the event from a different vantage point. It can be helpful to note (or speak aloud) your thoughts and then write or say them again in a different way, from a different perspective. Sometimes we need to loosen up our interpretive skills with a little creativity.

EMBRACE THE INNER AHA!—Learn to listen to your inner self—it knows the difference between clarity and confusion. An inner aha! may accompany sudden insights and feelings of deep connection. Pay attention. Strengthen your intuition and hone your interpretive abilities in order to know what is real.

SHADOW ANIMALS

A nother obstacle you might face when opening to animal teachers is bias. You request help and the animal that shows up is not one you are thrilled to encounter. For example, you do a meditation asking for insight and Snake appears. "Snake?" you think with disappointment. "I wanted an animal like Wolf or Lion, an animal that is noble or majestic. But Snake? Snakes are creepy. What could Snake show me?"

Shadow animals represent fears and reveal judgments.

And there's the bias—the surface projection that prevents you from seeing clearly and accepting the gift that is offered to you. Part of you may secretly hope that if you do the meditation again, a "better" animal will show up. This is how you close off experience and fail to discover what you really need to know.

ARE YOU READY?

Shadow animals appear when we are ready for their teachings. We may first be tested, or confronted with our own prejudices and fears. Shadow animals reveal our shadows—the lost, forgotten, or denied selves that exist deep down, beneath the veneer of who we present to the world.

To work with shadow animals, we must be willing to let go of expectations. We need to release our ideas of how we think things should be so that we can open ourselves to what is. We may be required to clear deep-rooted holds or mistaken beliefs.

So, how to begin? Perhaps we do some research on Snake. We learn that besides being one of the most feared animals on our planet, Snake is one of the most powerful and discerning of teachers. Snake doesn't appear to just anyone. Rather, Snake offers profound wisdom to the few who are willing to perceive beyond the surface.

When shadow animals show up, it's an invitation to look at our deep selves. It may be a challenge, for such teachings can reveal things we're not sure we want to see. And yet, this is precisely our treasure.

The following exercise invites you to explore some of your animal projections.

ANIMAL PROJECTIONS EXERCISE

1. Divide a journal page into four quadrants.

2. In the top left, list three of your favorite animal species—those you feel drawn to, connected with, or that you admire.

3. In the bottom left, list your three least favorite animals—those that you avoid, dislike, or that frighten you.

4. Now review your three favorite animal species. In the top right quadrant, jot down the qualities you like, admire, or find fascinating about these animals.

5. Do the same thing with your least favorite animals. Using the lower right quadrant, note the qualities that you most dislike or find frightening. Be honest; this is just for you.

6. Now breathe deeply and contemplate how all of the animal qualities you've listed on the right side of the paper may reflect aspects of yourself. Take your time and ponder deeply. The likes and dislikes we project onto animals are often the very qualities that we deny or fail to see and accept within ourselves.

Identifying what we most respect and admire or fear and avoid in animals can shed insight on our own inner strengths and weaknesses. We will explore this in the next exercise by journaling with a shadow animal guide.

When seen clearly, a shadow animal may become a powerful mentor.

JOURNALING WITH YOUR SHADOW ANIMAL

To begin, choose an animal that you fear or dislike. Find a quiet place to sit with your journal and writing instrument beside you. As you meditate, you'll also be taking notes.

1. Close your eyes, and use your breath to relax, center, and calm. [2 minutes.]

2. When ready, ask your animal to be present with you. Perhaps you see a grouping of animals in your mind's eye. Or perhaps one animal shows up as a representative for its species. Take several moments to tune in—feeling, seeing, and sensing that animal's energy. [2 minutes.]

3. Take a moment to jot down your first impressions. What do you sense about your animal? How do you feel in relation to it? [1 to 2 minutes.]

4. Thank your animal for connecting with you. Introduce yourself and let it know that you would like to learn more about working with shadow animals . . .

5. Just as you are able to sense your animal's energy, it can also sense yours. Ask your animal if it will give you some feedback on what it sees as your strengths and what you are doing well. You may get an image, a feeling, perhaps a phrase or an inner sense of knowing. Take a moment to write down what you perceive. [2 minutes.]

6. And now, ask your animal if it will comment on something it feels you might work on. Is there an area that could use help or be strengthened? Take a moment to listen and write down what you receive. [2 minutes.]

7. Lastly, ask your animal if it has a suggestion on something you can do to better understand its teaching. Perhaps you will receive an idea or an offer to help in the future. Whatever you sense, write it down now. [2 minutes.]

8. In closing, thank your animal for its insights, ideas, and suggestions. Thank it not just with words or thoughts, but with genuine feelings . . .

9. When you are ready, say goodbye to your animal and release your connection. Take a few deep breaths to clear your mind and bring your consciousness back to center.

JOURNAL PROMPTS

Take time to read your notes, adding
to them if needed. What did you
learn about this animal species?
Were you surprised by its energy and
interaction with you? What did you
feel when you first connected—and
did that change by the end of the
meditation? Do you sense that this
animal may have something to teach
you? Is this an animal you'd like
to work with in the future?
Why or why not?

CONSIDER EVERYTHING

Interpretation is an exercise in translation. It involves decoding symbolic images and uncovering signs to discover meaning. It requires us to be sensitive to thoughts and feelings that tug at our intuition. It is a game in noting unusual events and encounters, recognizing patterns, and identifying themes.

The more skilled we become in noticing the many ways our spirit animals communicate with us, the clearer the meaning and the easier we understand. So, how to begin? Here are ten steps to get you started.

1. TAKE INVENTORY—What do you already know and feel about this animal? Does the encounter spark a memory? Does it relate to recent events? Consider all that comes to mind.

2. RESEARCH—Gather facts about your animal's habits and habitat with books, articles, the Internet. Does your animal have any special abilities or unique skills? What triggers your interest?

3. OBSERVE—Watch and contemplate your animal's actions, mannerisms, and movements in nature. Use soft eyes (see page 34) to perceive beneath the surface. View wildlife films to watch your animal up close or in its native habitat.

4. LOOK FOR PATTERNS—Using your journal, look for recurring events with this animal. Has it appeared in other ways, at other times, or with other animals? Perhaps your current encounter is part of an ongoing theme? Be alert to repeating images, numbers, symbols, and correlating clues.

5. PAY ATTENTION TO DETAILS—Notice everything: objects, colors, actions, scenery, and background details. Think symbolically as well as literally. For example, a face-to-face encounter with an animal may mean you need to face something. Be alert to visual and verbal puns.

Rabbit can help us to uncover secrets and take intuitive leaps.

6. NOTE THE UNUSUAL—Notice what is odd or unexpected, and ponder its significance. For example, a human-sized rabbit may be alerting you to the great importance of its guidance, while a tiny rhinoceros may be indicating that only a little of its teaching is required.

7. CONSULT YOUR SHADOW—Are you minimizing something because you don't like it? Look at what makes you fearful, nervous, or uncertain in each event and encounter. Be willing to explore outside your comfort zone.

8. THINK OUTSIDE THE BOX—Some teachers manifest as extinct or mythic animals. Others might be wearing clothes. Don't dismiss the far-fetched. Instead, embrace these clues. Interpretation may require us to expand our outlook and consider meanings beyond the confines of ordinary reality.

9. BE WILLING TO SHIFT PERSPECTIVES—If you don't know what something means, seek meaning through a different perspective. For example, imagine yourself as your animal teacher. What would you be trying to tell yourself?

Some spirit animals use humor as a reminder to lighten up.

10. TRUST YOUR FEELINGS—First impressions, gut feelings, and hunches may be valid in themselves, or provide useful leads to other possibilities. Trust your feelings and consider everything!

In the following pages, we'll take a brief look at what colors, numbers, location, and actions or postures may represent in your animal encounters. These are jump starts to further investigation, designed to get creative juices flowing.

ANIMAL COLORS

An animal's color may symbolize its teaching. Additionally, unusual coloring (such as a dog with different-colored eyes), variance from reality (a green cow), and shifting colors may be clues to special skills.

WHITE

indicates clarity and transcendence. Spirit animals are often white, as are those that help us to travel between worlds or enter spiritual dimensions. White animals suggest wisdom, deep experience, and important quests.

BLACK

speaks to mystery and the unknown. Like white, black suggests profound knowledge and depth of experience. Black animals that journey or explore shadow realms can help you uncover that which is currently unknown.

GRAY

represents quiet composure and offers access to the in-between. Gray animals are often skilled in moving between dimensions. Their teachings may be subtle, vaporous, or hard to describe, but are powerfully transformational.

BLUE

is both sky and water, suggesting expansiveness, emotional depth, and sensitivity. Blue animals sometimes bring spiritual insights. Blue also connects to the throat chakra; animals with blue wings or throats can help to improve communication.

GREEN

is nature, new growth, and renewal. Green animals can signal new beginnings or projects. The heart chakra is green; animals with bright green eyes, scales, or feathers may offer assistance with healing and opening the heart.

GOLD

is about power, achievement, and abundance. Encountering a golden animal suggests accomplishment. You may be graduating from this animal's teaching, or advancing to a new level.

ANIMAL NUMBERS

The number of animals encountered may refer to the teaching theme, the amount of assistance available, or how far you've progressed.

ONE

is a starting point and window of opportunity. One animal means it is the main one, the only one for you to focus on at this time. It may lend clarity, strength, and insight, or propose a new adventure.

TWO

is about partnership and balance—male and female, yin and yang. A pair of animals can be polar opposites or a happy marriage of complements. Seeing two animals in succession can indicate emphasis, repetition, or the need for a double take.

THREE

is lucky, for three time's a charm. A group of three similar animals suggest inner lessons are moving along nicely. Three dissimilar animals (different in size or character, for instance) may indicate a need to harmonize before moving forward.

FOUR

shows stability, balance, and safety. Four animals of differing species may indicate your readiness to work with multiple guides and teachings. Four similar animals suggest quickening—and quadrupled energy now available to you.

FIVE

signals a challenge. A group of five animals may portend difficulties ahead but also equal opportunities for gain. Consult the group as well as each of the five for clues on how to proceed.

FLOCK, GROUP, PACK, OR HERD

Large gatherings of one animal family offer group energy and instruction in species teaching. Groups of multiple species reveal blended energies and may offer assistance in helping you to integrate a variety of teachings.

LOCATION

Physical location, landscape, and scenery can show where we are in relation to our animal's teaching. They may also signify where we are stuck, where we are going, and the area of consciousness currently explored.

LAND

references a stable, solid foundation. Land animals teach us how to be grounded and "down-to-earth." Animals that invite you underground may be asking you to pay attention to feelings or situations beneath the surface of consciousness. Insects and burrowing animals often provide expert insights in this area.

WATER

is fluid and flows easily; it is thus linked to the qualities and fluctuation of our emotions. Animal events occurring underwater may be directed to our subconscious or happening in our unconscious. Calm water reflects tranquillity while stormy waters denote turbulence in the emotional realm.

AIR

is symbolically linked with thoughts, intelligence, and spirit. Notice the quality of the air (is it foggy, cloudy, or polluted?) to ascertain if you need to perceive your animal's teaching more clearly. Creatures of the air may prompt us to see larger perspectives, elevate our thoughts, or connect with the spirit realm.

THE IN-BETWEEN

is represented by locations that separate or blend boundaries—often highlighting passage and transitional states of consciousness. A forest can suggest general inner-world exploration, while an island may indicate a self-contained, specific focus. Crossing a bridge implies change and movement, while ascending or descending a mountain speaks to the ups and downs of our journey.

ANIMAL POSTURES AND ACTIONS

What an animal is doing and how it is doing it offer clues to its style of teaching as well as our relationship to that teacher.

SITTING

indicates a grounded nature and a connection with the Earth. A sitting animal may hold its ground and be present for a time. Ask yourself: how does this animal's teaching sit with me?

STANDING

also suggests being grounded, but with an elevated perspective. Encountering a standing animal (especially one that does not usually stand) may be a hint that you need to look around and take a stand.

RUNNING

can mean enthusiasm or avoidance, depending on direction. An animal running toward you may be encouraging you to accept its teaching. Running after it can reveal eager willingness to follow its guidance. An animal chasing you suggests it's time to face what you've been avoiding, while running from it indicates a desire to evade.

FLYING

can represent freedom, spirit, and higher perspectives. Watching an animal fly may reveal a desire to soar above the ordinary. Are you ready to take flight? Flying with an animal suggests you are on your way to expanding awareness.

SLEEPING

often denotes tranquillity, trust, and patience. Observing a sleeping animal can mean its teaching is available to you but not yet awakened.

BITING

can be scary, but being bitten by an animal may also be an invitation to deeper teaching. In the shamanic world, such actions are sometimes seen as initiations to test one's ability to handle advanced aspects of an animal's guidance.

SAMPLE INTERPRETATION: HELLO BEAR!

L et's play with interpretation by taking a deeper look at an example from Chapter Two—"Hello Bear!" (see page 44). In this scenario you observe a bear tattoo on a stranger's arm. Later you notice a bear-paw pendant that your friend is wearing. And that evening you gaze at a large painting of a bear's face at a restaurant called Orso, which means "bear" in Italian.

Though you didn't encounter a physical bear, the spirit of Bear calls to you through this series of events. But what does it mean? Let's look at each encounter individually as well as their connections.

BEAR TATTOO

As wearable art, a tattoo represents creative self-expression. Because it is indelible, it also suggests permanence. You see the bear tattoo on a passing stranger. Perhaps you are still a stranger to Bear, familiar with its creative teaching only in passing. Yet, you notice the tattoo, suggesting you are alert to Bear in a peripheral way. The tattoo is on the stranger's arm. An arm suggests how we carry things or arm ourselves. Is this a hint to take hold of Bear's energy, to carry it (to bear it), or to arm yourself with its protection?

Be alert to puns: bear paws may signify a need to pause.

SILVER BEAR PAW

What does a paw bring to mind? The pendant is not a claw (which may indicate defense or protection) but a paw, denoting softness and sensitivity. Bears use their paws to travel. Could this single paw mean a step forward? Wearing it around the neck, upon the throat, links it with speech. Perhaps this placement suggests something about Bear that needs to be expressed?

LARGE PAINTING OF BEAR'S FACE

Gazing upon a larger-than-life face hints that something big—something worthy of your attention—is calling you to focus upon it in a personal way. Our face expresses our inner feelings and character. Something sizable and substantial within Bear is expressing itself to you. What is it you need to see or face in Bear?

A RESTAURANT CALLED BEAR

You discover that Orso—the name of the restaurant in which you are sitting — means "bear" in Italian. Orso and Bear are different words that represent the same animal. Is this a reflection? Consider this: you are sitting inside Orso, looking at a painting of Bear.

There's something funny here—you inside Bear, having a meal, as Bear faces you. Perhaps Bear is offering nourishment as well as companionship and a sense of humor.

PROGRESSION

The repetition of bear themes is more than coincidental. First on an arm, then on a neck, Bear appears to you one piece at a time. But soon you are face to face and symbolically inside of Bear. Your introduction to Bear is cumulative and quick. Perhaps its teaching is needed soon.

WHAT NOW?

Once an animal extends its offer to teach, it is your decision to accept or not. For ideas on accepting invitations and integrating animal guidance into your life, see Chapter Five.

YOUR DOG IS NOT MY DOG

A stray dog once crossed my path while I was walking with a friend. The dog was black and white, with floppy ears and a long thin tail. It paused as we came near. Cocking its head, it looked us up and down, then snorted softly and continued on its way. I laughed because the dog seemed comical in the way it regarded us—tilting its head as it assessed our presence, snorting as if finding us less than interesting. But my friend was not amused. She thought the dog was a warning, a reminder to be cautious when encountering strangers.

An animal can deliver different messages to different individuals.

On later contemplation, I found it fitting that the dog was black and white. My friend and I both saw the same dog at the same time, but had almost opposite experiences. What does it mean? The dog gave us each a reflective glimpse of our inner worldview while simultaneously demonstrating that interpretation is not as black and white as it may seem.

THE ART OF MANY TEACHINGS

Each animal species—as well as each individual animal—has a variety of qualities, skills, and areas of expertise. Because of this, every animal has several teachings.

When interpreting an animal's teaching, it's wise to avoid simplistic formulas of this equals that. Rather, the goal of interpretation is to determine which teaching is most relevant, appropriate, and meaningful for you.

Good interpretation is not so much a science as an art. Remember to engage both the intuitive dreamer and sharp-eyed detective as you play with interpretations. Value insights and intuitions from your right brain; welcome coherent connections and explanations from your left brain. Dance lightly as you discern deeper meanings and home in on what is most significant to your personal situation.

EMPOWER YOURSELF FIRST

The following chapter provides keys to 96 animal guides. Each profile explores several aspects of that animal's teaching, along with hints and questions for further exploration.

I know it can be tempting to immediately consult this section (or other books or Internet pages) for the "meaning" of an animal teacher. Before reading what others have written, however, I encourage you to contemplate your feelings and insights first. Ask yourself: what do I sense and know about this animal? What does this connection feel like to me? How does the experience touch my heart?

Once you have reviewed your own ideas, it can then be helpful to consider the thoughts of others. Animal-guide resources, such as the following chapter, are valuable in lending ideas, suggestions, and interpretive support.

They may confirm what you already know, as well as offer additional views about your animal, including perspectives that you may not yet have considered.

Make it a habit to consult yourself first. Use the insights of others to supplement your interpretations. Always consider what speaks most clearly and strongly to you. Welcome a variety of meanings. By empowering yourself you will strengthen your confidence, deepen your presence, and form a stronger relationship with your animal guide.

CHAPTER FOUR

THE KEY TO
SPIRIT ANIMALS
AND
THEIR TEACHINGS

⚷⟶ Familiarize yourself
with the teachings of
96 animal species

....

⚷⟶ Learn to align with your animal
guide's skills and perceptions

....

⚷⟶ Discover how to benefit from
every animal's expertise

....

⚷⟶ Question inner needs in
order to apply animal wisdom
more accurately to your life

LARGE MAMMALS

KEYS:

- ⚷ Strong and sensitive
- ⚷ Know how to endure
- ⚷ Loyal guardians
- ⚷ Attuned to Earth's heartbeat

BEAR: BLACK AND BROWN

KEYS

- Brave and resourceful
- Celebrates adventure
- Balances introspection with decisive action
- Instills confidence

TEACHING

Curious, intelligent, strong, and powerful, Bear is one of the first animals humans admired and worshipped. Bear is a warrior—courageous, self-confident, and skilled in defense.

While all bears share some general teachings (such as keeping healthy boundaries), each bear has its own area of expertise. Black Bear teaches resourcefulness and self-sufficiency, while Brown Bear encourages us to proclaim ourselves and take a stand. (See Panda Bear and Polar Bear, pages 70–71, for different bear teachings.) Both black and brown bears sleep through the winter and awaken in spring. Bear understands the art of timing and encourages us to nurture our creative ideas until they are ready to be expressed to the world. A helpful dreamtime advisor, Bear knows the value of introspection and searching for wisdom within.

Highly inquisitive and humorous at times, bears can be mischievous. No stranger to fun and adventure, Bear is an exuberant guide to inner-world explorations.

QUESTIONS

Does your confidence need a boost? Are you standing up for yourself? Or, are you being too assertively bearish with those around you? Bear is a master of balance and can help both to bolster boldness and to tame aggressive tendencies. Bear appreciates genuine seekers who are willing to work for their answers. Are you ready to bare it all? Invite Bear to your dreams and ask: what is it I need to know?

BEAR: PANDA

Though mostly easygoing and carefree, pandas are loners. Roaming through vast bamboo forests in remote mountainous regions, they are sensitive to noise and the intrusion of others. Panda reminds us to take our time, enjoy our own company, and be at home in the tranquil surroundings of nature.

In Eastern traditions, Panda is a good luck symbol of peace and harmony. Perhaps this is because Panda moves slowly and focuses on one thing at a time. Watch Panda to learn more about the elegance of simplicity. Panda advocates a calm lifestyle that values patience, contentment, and quiet wandering.

KEYS

○—► Balances strength with sensitivity
○—► Treasures solitude and tranquillity
○—► Advises good personal boundaries
○—► Represents peace and harmony

TEACHING

We are easily charmed by the teddy-bear quality of pandas. Their soft, furry, rounded appearance draws us in, as do their stylish black and white markings. Still, pandas are bears and know how to engage their warrior nature if need be. This is a key to Panda's teaching: how to balance a gentle soul with effective personal boundaries.

QUESTIONS

Are you overly sensitive? Continually riding up and down an emotional rollercoaster that never seems to end? Take a Zen break with Panda—breathe deep and slow down. Find balance by nurturing yourself with beauty and what you love. By learning to say no to that which is not nourishing, you may begin to recognize the healthy abundance that is all around you. Call upon Panda to express yourself firmly yet gently.

BEAR: POLAR

KEYS

- Strong, powerful, intrepid
- Respected spirit guide
- Accomplished dreamtime traveler
- Serious nature tempered with curiosity and humor

TEACHING

As the largest and strongest of bears, and the only one living at the top of the world, Polar Bear is a formidable teacher. Highly respected by ancient shamans of the Far North, Polar Bear connects deeply with land, ice, sea, and sky, offering exceptional guidance through a variety of worlds.

Whether stalking seals on ice floes, roaming barren, snow-covered lands, or diving through frigid seas, polar bears rely on finely tuned observational skills and adapt to their environment. A nomadic, experienced traveler and excellent swimmer, Polar Bear can help us navigate emotional realms with strength and purpose.

While all bears have a paw in dreaming, Polar Bear is the most accomplished, with special skills in lucid dreaming. Polar Bear knows how to trek alone through the polar night and is thus an excellent companion when exploring mystical realms of consciousness.

Like most bears, Polar Bear is intelligent, curious, and intuitive. Fearless and sometimes fierce, Polar Bear also has a dry sense of humor.

QUESTIONS

Are you on the brink of something big and powerful? Has your search brought you close—but not quite close enough—to enlightenment? Call upon the great white bear to traverse final obstacles and complete a long-term spiritual quest. If you are ready to make a breakthrough, some reliable counsel and robust guidance from Polar Bear may be just what you need.

BISON/BUFFALO

KEYS

- Represents abundance
- Gives freely
- Lives in accordance with nature
- Respects all life
- Reminds us to give thanks and be grateful

TEACHING

Symbol of gratitude, generosity, and service, powerful Bison understands the value of sacrifice to feed and clothe others. Under Bison's tutelage, we learn to give thanks, respect life, and honor the spirits of animals that feed and clothe us.

Bison enjoy open spaces and love to roam freely. Let your inner Bison roam free to reconnect with the Earth and recognize the divine nature in all beings. Bison reminds us to see the good in life and be thankful for what we have.

At well over 1,000 pounds, Bison is a physical representation of abundance. Large, stable, solid, Bison reminds us that we are provided for. More than that, Bison reveals how we can lighten up and flow with life, carry burden without complaint, and live well with dignity and confidence.

Call on Bison when starting new projects or endeavors. Bison advises us not to hurry or force things, but to remain grounded, stay true to ourselves, and follow our path with integrity. This is how we can manifest our dreams.

QUESTIONS

Are you grateful for what you have? If so, have you been giving thanks? Bison says, acknowledge your blessings, for the Earth is plentiful. Cultivate appreciation and share your sentiments with others. Forget complaining. Rather than finding fault, see what's good and true. That's how you join Bison in celebrating abundance.

CAMEL

KEYS

- O⊸ Knows how to adapt
- O⊸ Guides through challenging journeys
- O⊸ Advocates self-reliance
- O⊸ Helps us to go the distance

TEACHING

Imagine a long line of camels, bundled with human provisions, trekking day after day through scorching heat, relentless sandstorms, and constantly shifting dunes. This is a good image of Camel's teaching: helping us to survive adversity and successfully travel through harsh environments with persistence and endurance.

Camels have been masters at long-distance travel since ancient times. By storing fat in their humps, they can draw upon inner reserves and regulate their metabolism. With long, protective eyelashes and nostrils that close against blowing sand, camels know how to persevere—and complete a journey that others may fail or abandon.

Camel never gives up, patiently encouraging us to keep on keeping on—calmly, consistently, steadfastly. The reward at the end of the journey? An oasis of bright opportunities, helpful connections, and newfound possibilities.

The long haul may be tough, but Camel gets us to where we need to be.

QUESTIONS

Are you running on empty? Does your soul feel parched? Do you fear the challenges of a daunting quest ahead? Camel's calm guidance can help you stay positive, even during arduous situations. By helping us to find and utilize inner resources, Camel inspires us to persevere. You are stronger than you know. Align with Camel and you may trust that it will all work out in the end.

COW

KEYS
- Exhibits peace and contentment
- Nurtures through maternal love
- Advises sharing
- Helps us to see the goodness of life

TEACHING

Look into a cow's soulful eyes and you may glimpse the gentle intelligence and quiet wisdom that resides within. Cows don't need to be loud or show off because they know—and are content with—who they are. This is one of Cow's grand teachings: to appreciate and love ourselves just as we are.

In ancient times, Cow was worshipped as the Great Mother. Provider of life-giving milk, Cow symbolized fertility, motherhood, and abundance. Cows are good mothers, nourishing their young not only with sustenance, but protection and guidance. Cow offers maternal advice, reminding us to lovingly support both our children and our creative projects so they will grow to be happy and healthy.

Cow also encourages us to ruminate on our experiences—to thoroughly digest each bit of wonder and joy in the world. Slow down, says Cow; feel your feet on the earth and the nourishing energies that support you. Cow reminds us that life is good.

QUESTIONS

Do you appreciate the joy of simple pleasures? Do you feel connected with the bright green pastures of your being? Are you nourishing yourself well? If the answer to any of these questions is no, go sit with Cow. Right now. Smell her sweet, earthy scent, lose yourself in her loving eyes, drink in the rich nourishment of her presence. Cow offers comfort and reassurance that all is well.

DEER

KEYS

- O—⚲ Skilled listener
- O—⚲ Teaches empathy
- O—⚲ Excellent guide for children
- O—⚲ Powerful yet gentle healer

TEACHING

Sometimes linked with the fairy realm, Deer is graceful, delicate, and serene. But Deer also knows some secrets. Ancient peoples used to follow deer to find the best herbs and medicinal plants. This is one of Deer's teachings—to help us heal by locating restorative treasures within.

Deer are watchful, alert to danger, and skilled in hiding. They know how to move quietly and observe keenly, often seeing and hearing what others cannot. Particularly good at journeying through daydreams and meditations, Spirit of Deer can lead us to restful, healing spaces in our inner landscape.

There is an innocence about Deer—an openhearted quality that encourages appreciation of nature's beauty and acceptance of self. Deer guides gently and calmly, and for this reason works well with children and sensitive individuals. Kind and benevolent, Deer teaches empathy in an elegant manner. Sometimes linked to happiness and good fortune, Deer's teaching is simple and honest.

QUESTIONS

Are you in need of some deep yet tender healing? Deer offers empathy and compassionate care. Breathe deep, cry if you need to, and unburden yourself. Deer listens well, and can help to relieve the devastation of trauma or a broken heart. Deer will help you find and reclaim your inner child with a gentle touch. Pause as you look in the mirror, says Deer. You are more beautiful than you know.

ELEPHANT

KEYS

- Patient, loyal, wise
- Engages life with sensitivity
- Values commitment
- Nurtures compassion

TEACHING

Solid, stable, intelligent, and often quite determined, Elephant is known to discern clearly and remember well. You can't fool an elephant. Linked in ancient times to royalty and wisdom, Elephant can be a true and loyal friend.

While elephants don't see well, they are sensitive in other ways. Herds use low-frequency sounds to communicate over far distances. Elephant is particularly skilled in listening and can help us hear our inner voice, develop telepathic skills, and comprehend what others really mean, despite what they may say.

Living in matriarchal groups, elephants form deep bonds. Elephant teaches loyalty and reminds us to cherish all family members. Despite their large size, mother elephants use gentle guidance to nurture compassion in young, sensitive souls. Elephant encourages us to be fair and just, and live in harmony with nature.

Elephants display a wide range of emotions, including love and sorrow. Perceptive and purposeful, Elephant can help to unearth hidden memories as well as trauma that needs to be healed.

QUESTIONS

Are you angry at how life is treating you? Do you feel there's no justice in the world? Elephant invites you to uncover the more vulnerable emotions you may be hiding beneath anger and outrage. Elephant nudges us to recognize the truth within ourselves in a gentle, loving way. By doing so, we learn to be more gentle and loving with others.

GIRAFFE

KEYS

- Bridges worlds
- Represents grounded yet expansive viewpoints
- Advises quiet contemplation
- Encourages us to reach our potential

TEACHING

The most noticeable thing about a giraffe—its long, supple neck—is also a symbol of its teaching. Giraffe bridges worlds: the ground below with the sky above; earth-based knowledge with expansive views; a grounded presence with vantage points that allow perception into the distance and the future.

Giraffe's neck (composed of seven vertebrae, just like ours) is elegant, strong, and flexible. Giraffe encourages us to look around and consider all points of view before taking action. Peering over treetops, giraffes know in advance what's coming toward them and where to move next. Giraffe models how to use expanded awareness in safe, practical ways.

Giraffes are quiet, using body movements to communicate with others. Giraffe teaches attention to detail and visual cues. You may not need words to communicate when a simple gesture or expression can say so much more. Giraffe encourages us to simplify, to refrain from over-explanation or expressing ourselves too loudly. Quiet contemplation yields deep wisdom of self.

QUESTIONS

Are you feeling small and ineffective? Are you limiting yourself to only one point of view? Perhaps it's time to stick your neck out and consider other options. Giraffe can help you stretch beyond self-imposed beliefs and restrictions. With Giraffe's supportive guidance, you may find poise and stability through inner balance. You may also discover that you can reach higher than you think you can.

GORILLA

KEYS

- Solid, stable, gentle, kind
- Champions fairness
- Teaches respect and love through peaceful living
- Inspires honesty, dignity, and soul presence

TEACHING

Though large and powerfully built, the mighty gorilla is surprisingly calm and gentle. Shy, thoughtful, and sensitive to group dynamics, Gorilla encourages us to move past surface impressions in order to know the real being within.

Gorillas share well and are extremely loyal, caring for and protecting family members, especially the young and old. The troop is led by a strong male who balances authority with respect and fairness to all. Gorilla teaches us how to behave honorably, with dignity, integrity, and compassion.

Communicating with a wide range of sounds and gestures, gorillas are attentive and attuned to nuance. Soulful and pensive, Gorilla brings healing by listening and accepting. Firmly connected to Earth energies, Gorilla knows how to be fully present. This magnificent great ape is not just intelligent, but wise.

QUESTIONS

Do you feel pushed around or bullied by others? Or are you the one doing the pushing? We are often quick to cover feelings of fear and anger with an urge to control others. Is that what's at the core of your imbalance? Don't worry. Gorilla's gentle nature is healing in itself. Sit with Gorilla to access deeper feelings and perceive the truth. Speak gently and honestly—with yourself and with others—and act with compassion. Gorilla can help you find the noble leader within.

HORSE

KEYS

- ⚬━ Awakens adventure
- ⚬━ Opens the heart
- ⚬━ Encourages passion and joy

TEACHING

With beauty and grace, Horse inspires us to experience the joy of movement as our spirit gallops to its destiny. In mythic tales, horses may have immense wings or a magical horn, signifying the power of flight and heightened awareness. Horse is a faithful inner guide, encouraging the thrill of freedom and spirit of adventure that accompanies flying through astral realms. Horse can help expand intuitive awareness and bring psychic abilities to consciousness.

Friendly and free-spirited, yet proud and powerful, Horse nudges us to open our heart in order to join with others in love and partnership. Horse teaches balance between freedom and responsibility, adventure and belonging, personal power and group harmony. Horse encourages trust, mutual respect, and a deeper awareness of how we may work together for a common good. With Horse we learn to appreciate the magnitude and majesty of our soul's journey in the company of others.

QUESTIONS

Horse often speaks to movement, balance, and inner freedom. Do you feel constricted? Do you need to move in a new direction? Are you being held back by others—or are you doing the holding? Horse loves to run wild and free but is also sensitive to the needs of others. Take care to balance the fervor of freedom with introspection. Here's a key question: Is my heart open to all? Horse senses our deep emotions and can help.

KANGAROO

KEYS

- o—🖈 Leaps forward
- o—🖈 Knows how to balance and counterbalance
- o—🖈 Brings change and adventure
- o—🖈 Jumps for joy

TEACHING

With long, powerful legs and strong tails that help them to balance, kangaroos are designed to leap! For Kangaroo, jumping is a joy—the momentum, height, and distance speak to forward movement that is easy, graceful, and fun.

Kangaroos know when to leap away from dangerous situations, and they only leap forward. Spirit of Kangaroo teaches us to listen to our instincts and act quickly when immediate action is required. Kangaroo focuses on moving ahead, never back.

The length and strength of their tails allow kangaroos to counterbalance in any direction—a subtle yet powerful move. Kangaroo can teach us how to fall back on ourselves in order to balance any situation.

Kangaroos also have good focus and clarity. Working with Kangaroo may require eliminating mental clutter to clear the path ahead for change and adventure. When traveling for long periods of time, Kangaroo can be a helpful guide to leap over obstacles and carry on.

QUESTIONS

If Kangaroo comes to you, change may be imminent. Are you ready to leap far and high? Kangaroo offers assistance to go the distance, but you must be willing to jump—perhaps into the unknown. You will learn many things: how to adapt, welcome new situations, and rely on your inner self in times of confusion. If you are willing to give it your all, you may leap to success with Kangaroo.

LLAMA

KEYS

- Natural healer
- Balances grounded knowledge with expanded awareness
- Stimulates telepathy and spiritual connections
- Aligns and harmonizes energy

TEACHING

Living at elevated altitudes in mountainous regions, llamas are naturally attuned to high frequencies of energy. Sensible, intuitive, and intelligent, they remain centered and grounded as they stimulate the expansion of awareness. Like reception antennas, they can help us tune in to spiritual wavelengths that offer health, wisdom, and inner development.

Llamas are curious and know the value of seeking. Spirit of Llama reminds us to use our intuition when following the subtle energies that call to us. Sure-footed llamas travel confidently through narrow mountain passes. Llama guides us in the right direction and can help us feel secure as we explore different frequencies, energy patterns, and inner dimensions.

Llamas hum to communicate a variety of feelings, and use telepathy to stay connected. Devoted and caring, llamas value each herd member for its unique area of expertise. Llamas are experts at harmonizing group energies, ensuring that each individual, as well as the herd, is happy and healthy.

QUESTIONS

Are you singing in tune? Is your outlook one of harmony and equilibrium? If not, call on Llama for a simple yet skilled adjustment. It could sound like this: hmmmmmmm. You may not even know Llama is helping but suddenly you feel better, lighter, happier. Llama knows how to align discordant energy patterns so they flow smoothly and in harmony. Subtle yet powerful is Llama's healing tone.

LION

KEYS

- Noble leader
- Symbol of inner strength
- Inspires self-respect
- Invokes courage

TEACHING

Associated with the sun, gold, and royalty, Lion reminds us to remember who we are and conduct ourselves with dignity. Leading firmly, with a noble heart, Lion can help us to express our inner authority in a way that is commanding but not domineering.

In the wild, young lions learn to be brave by challenging each other and by observing their elders. Lions know when to play and when to relax, when to wait and when to spring into action. Spirit of Lion teaches responsibility to family, loyalty to community, and the importance of restful contemplation in order to make wise, grounded decisions.

Graceful and stealthy, lions strengthen their spirit through experience and daring. Lion is vigilant, and can be fierce, but knows the importance of a calm, cool exterior.

Lion has some powerful knowledge but doesn't give it away for free. Are you willing to work? Lion requires attentiveness and commitment. In return, Lion may help you strengthen your dignity and find nobility within.

QUESTIONS

Are you worn down from too much work? Do you feel overwhelmed by deadlines? Are your emotions frayed from an unending blur of busyness? Lion advises that the best way to continue is to relax and de-stress fully. So drop what you're doing, take a rest and listen to Lion's first lesson: you can't expect to do things well if you don't treat yourself with care and respect.

MOOSE

KEYS
- Patient and persistent
- Connects deeply with the Earth
- Teaches self-reliance
- Finds wisdom in nature

TEACHING
Moose is a symbol of perseverance and endurance. Though they are quite large and appear ungainly, these animals are surprisingly agile and speedy. It's easy to misjudge Moose. The largest members of the deer family, they are both hardy and sensitive.

Usually quiet and unassuming, moose will stomp and snort loudly when threatened. They know how to stand their ground and will defend, especially if calves are present. Moose knows the value of camouflage and silent observation, but advocates strong action when necessary.

Moose forage widely and have a knack for finding food even in deep snow and harsh weather. They sometimes submerge their great heads into ponds to eat water plants—a reminder to look beneath the surface for nourishment.

Moose wander alone or with calves, never in herds. Self-reliant and assured, Spirit of Moose invites us to deepen our connections with nature and the Earth. Moose knows that what we need is all around us. It is up to us to look and listen and learn.

QUESTIONS
Are you feeling a bit lost? Not quite sure what you want—or if you have the energy to find out? Take a walk with Moose. It may not seem as if you're doing much of anything, but Moose can help you gain confidence and direction. Journey beside Moose to soak in Earth's energy and discover more about who you are.

PUMA

(COUGAR, PANTHER, AND MOUNTAIN LION)

KEYS

o—⊷ Fine-tunes perception
o—⊷ Cuts through illusions
o—⊷ Opens awareness to spirit world
o—⊷ Clarifies and integrates

TEACHING

With an extensive range of habitat, this tawny-colored, erect-eared, long-tailed cat is known by different names in different places—puma, cougar, panther, and mountain lion.

Large yet lithe, pumas move swiftly and silently, with stealth. They know when to hide and when to act. Pumas advance intuitively, abruptly changing direction when necessary. Spirit of Puma is a consummate guide to inner-world journeying, encouraging us to steer clear of illusions, move toward clarity, and leap when the time is right.

Pumas feel vibrations through their whiskers, and have keen visual, smelling, and hearing abilities. Puma can help fine-tune all our senses so that we may perceive in sharper, clearer ways. Long-term work with Puma may stimulate awareness of the spirit realm.

Puma understands how to reclaim power and use it wisely, especially during times of transformation. Puma pushes us to integrate what we've learned. An accomplished, no-nonsense teacher, Puma can help us achieve self-actualization with catlike precision.

QUESTIONS

Are you caught in the turmoil of emotional upheaval? Does your heart pitter-patter with fear, angst, or uncertainty? Puma offers clarity through confusion and chaos by helping you to see what is real and what is not—and to move forward in an elegant, balanced way. There are no shortcuts when working with Puma, and the terrain may be difficult, but lessons learned are for a lifetime.

REINDEER/CARIBOU

KEYS
- Strong and fast
- Travel far
- Family oriented
- Teaches adaptation

TEACHING

Reindeer (semi-domesticated caribou) have been helping humans since ancient times. Noble animals, they represent wisdom, endurance, and creative adaptation. Family oriented, they welcome social interaction within the herd and with humans. Spirit of Reindeer nudges us to find our place in large groups, and can help to harmonize communication.

Reindeer live in extremely cold terrain. Like deer and moose, they know how to find food even under packed snow. Reindeer teaches inner strength, perseverance, and how to adapt when things get tough. Reindeer sense keenly and accurately assess their surroundings. They know what needs to be done and how to do it.

Both male and female reindeer may have antlers. Reindeer knows how to balance masculine and feminine energies, and how to temper each.

Reindeer are good swimmers and fast runners, and often travel far. Some migrations cover over 3,000 miles. When moving or traveling, Reindeer is an excellent companion. When the journey seems too hard, Reindeer reminds you that you have the fortitude to succeed.

QUESTIONS

If Reindeer comes to you, it may be time to question your place in the herd. How well do you work with others? Do you need to take charge, or do you need to follow? Reindeer reminds us to honor both group dynamics and personal needs. Invite Reindeer to share creative ideas on how to balance and harmonize.

RHINOCEROS

KEYS

- Values solitude
- Roams open spaces
- Discerns truth
- Advocates self-knowledge

TEACHING

Though their large, solid bodies are well armored with thick skin, rhinoceroses are surprisingly sensitive. With excellent senses of smell, hearing, and intuition, they are also skilled in assessing situations accurately. Rhino suggests that we take in all the knowledge that our senses share.

Grounded, balanced, close to the earth, rhinoceroses are most often passive and peaceful, roaming alone through open, grassy plains. Rhinos enjoy solitude and take care to maintain good personal boundaries. Rhino can help us not only to feel comfortable being alone, but to genuinely enjoy solitude.

Sometimes known for their aggressive tendencies, rhinos will charge if frightened or threatened. Rhino reminds us to be open to life but to protect ourselves as well.

Highly treasured and often coveted by humans, rhinoceros horn symbolizes the perception of truth—to know who you are. But Rhino's horn belongs to Rhino. You can never know yourself by poaching truth; rather, you must find it within yourself. Rhino recommends self-knowledge as the path to wisdom.

QUESTIONS

Are you overly sensitive—or not sensitive enough? Do you shun others or crave constant company? Is there too much distance—or not enough—between yourself and others? Roam with Rhino to find a happy balance of calm inner contentment and joyful interaction with the world. Rhino reminds us that that we already know the answers. Rhino's recommendation: go within and listen to your wise inner self.

TIGER

KEYS
⦿⟶ Acts with precision
⦿⟶ Instills confidence
⦿⟶ Deepens presence
⦿⟶ Awakens passion and power

TEACHING

Prowling silently through the dark of night, the largest of all cat species moves with purpose and self-assurance. Tiger knows the power of stealth—and surprise. Hidden within its furry paws are razor-sharp claws that spring to readiness when the time is right. Supremely focused and highly attuned to everything in its environment, Tiger knows how to act with precision.

There's nothing wishy-washy about Tiger's teaching. Indeed, when Tiger appears, it's time to get serious. Tiger teaches us to pay attention to small details—gestures, movements—while maintaining full awareness of the surrounding jungle. No small feat!

Physically strong and streamlined, tigers know the range of their power. Their senses are keen, their movements assertive and commanding, yet fluid and responsive too. Tiger's stripes symbolize a strongly balanced composure. Tiger helps us to move and act with greater self-assurance by reminding us of our own inner strength. Watching Tiger is a lesson in how to integrate intensity with sensitivity, power with poise.

QUESTIONS

Are your actions ineffective or unconvincing? Do you fail to impress? Or, are you overbearingly arrogant and dismissive of others? In either case, you may benefit from Tiger's assistance. As you learn to own and express your power in a balanced way, you will assert yourself calmly and confidently, without bravado or excess humility. If you want to be the big cat of the jungle, take a hint from Tiger.

WOLF

KEYS

- ⚷ Symbol of the wild
- ⚷ Free spirit
- ⚷ Dedicated to pack and family
- ⚷ Skilled in strategy
- ⚷ Teaches wisdom through experience

TEACHING

Fiercely independent yet extremely loyal to their pack and cubs, wolves balance free-spirited adventures with faithfulness and responsibility. Strong and intelligent, they avoid fighting but will stand their ground. Wolf teaches respect of self with fairness and dedication to community.

Clever and canny, wolves know how to strategize and work together well. Howling in unison, hunting in packs—they understand and celebrate social rituals. Spirit of Wolf connects us with the Earth and cycles of change.

Wolf encourages us to learn through experience and act with integrity. Working with Wolf can be demanding and is often a long-term process. Wolf requires focus and dedication, pushing us to see what is, rather than be clouded by how we want things to be. Wolf teaches with a fierce and honest love, for its hard lessons are aimed toward the shining self it knows we can become.

QUESTIONS

Have you lost your way? Is your mind bewildered, with no idea what you're doing or where you're headed? Wolf's teaching may be just the ticket to gain some confidence and direction. Wolf is particularly astute in identifying inner strengths and reminds us to always trust our instincts. Wolf may challenge you to face your fears—including, perhaps, the reason for your current confusion. Wolf pushes us to know our true selves so that we may discover the path we need to follow.

ZEBRA

KEYS
- Teaches acceptance
- Evokes compassion
- Celebrates individuality
- Harmonizes group energy

TEACHING

As members of the horse family, zebras are distinct. Every black and white stripe on every zebra in every herd is also distinct—an excellent metaphor for Zebra's teaching. Though zebras rely upon group dynamics for survival, they equally honor the individual views and talents of each herd member. Zebra teaches the power of belonging wholeheartedly to a group without losing one's sense of self.

Fast and agile, zebras are accomplished at moving quickly in the midst of confusion. Zebra can thus help you to stay focused even when chaos is all around you.

Zebra advises integrating energies— male and female, dark and light, known and unknown—so that we may experience life in larger ways. In Zebra's world, things are not so much black or white, but black and white. Move past rigid viewpoints that separate and divide, says Zebra. Rather, observe the complement of contrast, celebrate variety, and embrace a plurality of views.

QUESTIONS

Is your world characterized by an "us versus them" mentality? Or is it just yourself against the world? Perhaps you need some time with Zebra. Under Zebra's wise and calming influence you may begin to experience the profound beauty of diversity. With a gentle nudge to open the heart, Zebra reminds us that we are all part of a planetary family— each one of us quirky and talented and deserving of love; each and every one an essential part of the whole.

SMALL MAMMALS

KEYS

- Adventurous
- Clever and curious
- Attentive to detail
- Alert to opportunity
- Grounded and connected to the Earth

BADGER

KEYS

- Tenacious
- Communes with Earth wisdom
- Gets to the core of things
- Champions self-expression

TEACHING

Sometimes known as the keeper of stories, Badger likes to burrow deep, commune with the Earth, and contemplate its ancient tales. Persistent and practical, badgers dig down and root around beneath the surface, often creating a maze of tunnels. Badger can help us explore vast territories of our inner world, and uncover the secrets and treasures hidden within.

Small, bold, and fearless, badgers can be aggressive if threatened and ferocious when fighting. With strong jaws and sharp claws, badgers know how to defend. While their eyesight is not strong, they have keen senses of smell and hearing. Spirit of Badger is good at sensing energy and asserting what it wants. Likewise, Badger encourages us to express ourselves and let others know our point of view.

A discerning and highly respected teacher, Badger has no time for half-hearted students. Working with Badger requires respect and willingness to persist. Badger is quite tenacious and you may discover that a little of its energy goes a very long way.

QUESTIONS

Do you fail to stand up for yourself, make your views known, or fight for what you want? Are you expressing yourself at all? Welcome Badger for some straightforward lessons in speaking up, announcing yourself, and asking for what you need. Badger can help you speak honestly and assertively, without backing down. With Badger beside you, communicative confidence is solid and assured.

BAT

KEYS

- At home in the dark
- Skilled in flight and perception
- Helpful to the Earth
- Initiates deep change

TEACHING

Humans often misunderstand bats. Perhaps it is because bats are so unusual. Hanging upside down in caves, cloaked inside their large leathery wings, bats seem dead to the world—until night approaches. Bats are the only mammals that can fly and have unique abilities to "see" in the dark.

Most bats live in huge colonies. Highly social with strong family ties, they have a loving, gentle touch. They also do a lot of good for the Earth. Bats pollinate plants, eat insects, and provide guano, an excellent fertilizer. People who fear bats often fear change and their own shadowy realm of subconscious fears—addressing these aspects is part of Bat's teaching.

Contrary to popular belief, bats are not blind; they can actually see better than humans. They also use high-frequency sounds to skillfully navigate through the dark. Bat can help us to travel through unfamiliar territory, perceive in more sensitive ways, appreciate new perspectives, and strengthen our intuition.

QUESTIONS:

On the brink of change? Ready for a dramatic shift? Are you excited, but a little fearful too? Bat is a great initiator, often attendant to the ending of one phase of life and the beginning of another. Bat knows the value of inner preparation. Hang with Bat to release old fears and aspects of self that no longer serve. Wise and discerning, Bat is an excellent facilitator of deep and lasting change.

BEAVER

KEYS
- Creative builder
- Values home and family
- Teaches pride in craftsmanship
- Blends form and function

TEACHING

Persistent and industrious, with admirable work ethics, beavers are master builders. Their dams can change the flow of rivers and the contours of land. Both astute and practical, beavers survey their environment for building resources, then set to work. Beaver teaches us how to focus our efforts, use materials at hand, and work hard in order to achieve our goals.

While quite productive, beavers are also devoted to their families. They create secure, comfortable lodges and include their young in building activities. Beavers work well together and know how to divide tasks efficiently. They are also clever, patiently working through obstacles by implementing creative alternatives. Beavers value form as well as function. Their lodges and dams are not only constructed carefully with strong foundations, but artfully, with good attention to detail. Spirit of Beaver acknowledges accomplishment and encourages us to take pride in our work, to love and protect our creations.

QUESTIONS:

Are you stuck in the middle of a creative endeavor? Or do you need inspiration to start something new? Call upon Beaver for some down-to-earth ideas that will stimulate the flow of enthusiasm and help you find your artistic groove. Beaver may encourage you to integrate creativity with practicality, resulting in works that are not only beautiful but useful too. Working with Beaver ensures that everything fits together just so.

CAT

KEYS

- ⦵⟶ Independent and self-assured
- ⦵⟶ Intuitive and insightful
- ⦵⟶ Agile and astute

TEACHING

Known as a goddess in ancient Egypt, Cat is a creature of mystery and majesty. Humans have long associated Cat with magic, shape-shifting, and mystical knowledge, as well as secrets, darkness, and superstition. Intuitive and intelligent, Cat is a free-thinking, creative spirit, generally indifferent to human opinion.

Cat teaches independence, resourcefulness, and self-reliance. Swift and nimble, cats move gracefully, skillfully—stalking with stealth, leaping with confidence. Cat champions an agile body and discerning mind. As a teacher, Cat can help us move quickly, see clearly, and make unexpected breakthroughs. Insightful and self-assured, Cat speeds up the process of self-discovery.

Comfortable in shadows, cats like to prowl at night, exploring that which is not often seen by others. Not afraid of the dark—or a challenge—Cat offers unique perspectives as it nudges us to explore inner realms. An accomplished and discerning power animal, Cat can help us confront our fears, heighten our intuitive abilities, and move both assertively and stylishly through unfamiliar territory.

QUESTIONS

Need some confidence? Or clarity? Whether napping in the sunshine or journeying through the shadow realm, you'll learn some secrets of self-assurance and perspicuity by spending time with Cat. Cat's teaching is often one of presence, so pay attention to subtle cues and feelings. Move sensuously, perceive deeply, and awaken your inner feline. Once you do, you will never take any cat for granted.

COYOTE

KEYS
- Wise trickster
- Inventive, clever, and cunning
- Alert to opportunity
- Balances wisdom with humor

TEACHING
In Native American legends, Coyote is the great trickster who causes mischief, exposes self-deception, and reminds us to laugh. Smart and cunning with a sharp wit and skilled flair for humor, Coyote encourages us to embrace our foibles as a prelude to change.

Adventurous, curious, and extremely clever, Coyote may seem only to want fun and excitement. But coyotes in the wild are practical as well. Very loyal, they mate for life and have close families. Fast runners, good hunters, and keenly attuned to their environment, coyotes know how to adapt—and survive.

Linked to creativity and new beginnings, Coyote attempts to free us from self-limiting beliefs so that we can grow. Sniff out new opportunities, says Coyote. Don't take things too seriously, and always welcome your sense of humor. Using laughter to stimulate larger ways of thinking, Coyote encourages a joyful heart and open mind.

QUESTIONS
What is your secret heart's desire—and what stands in the way of you achieving it? Intelligent and insightful, Coyote can help you identify the core fear that is holding you back from finding true happiness. Coyote has an unconventional but extremely effective approach. With Coyote you might not only learn to see outside the box, but to jump—to be daring and seize opportunity and embrace what you really want. Howl regularly with Coyote and life will bring you what you need.

DOG

KEYS

○⊶ Faithful friend
○⊶ Models selfless service
○⊶ Enjoys simple pleasures
○⊶ Loves unconditionally

TEACHING

Reliable, trustworthy, loving, and loyal—first and foremost, Dog is a friend. Symbols of devotion, dogs are our allies, companions, and so much more.

With sensitive smell and hearing abilities, dogs alert us to danger or intrusion. They watch and guard, herd and hunt, and assist the vision- and hearing-impaired. Search dogs find us, rescue dogs aid us, and sled dogs help us travel. Attentive to our physical and emotional needs, dogs protect us, amuse us, inspire us, and understand us. Spirit of Dog sets a shining example of selfless service.

Dogs are devoted to family—both their own and ours. Dogs help us to enjoy simple pleasures—a walk, a treat, a cuddle. Dogs make us laugh and entice us to play, encouraging us to lighten up and have some fun. Dog softens our heart and heals us simply by being near. By loving us so wholeheartedly, Dog encourages us to love ourselves as well.

QUESTIONS

More than anything, Dog is a true friend. What about you? Dog mirrors our personality, showing us what we most need to see. Are you loyal and kind? Do you need to wag your tail and have some fun? With a playful nature and engaging spirit, Dog heals and teaches that simple kindness is more powerful than control. Dog is everywhere—a great, noble teacher that looks into our soul and loves us, unconditionally.

FOX

KEYS

- ○⊶ Clever and quick-witted
- ○⊶ Values the art of timing
- ○⊶ Thinks outside the box
- ○⊶ Alerts us to magic

TEACHING

With a quick wit and spirited sense of adventure, Fox is always up for exploration. Clever and perceptive, Fox knows the value of investigation and encourages us to examine life with eyes of wonder. As a student of Fox, you may learn to sharpen your senses and sniff out new opportunities in order to more fully experience and appreciate the world.

Generally solitary, silent, and nocturnal, foxes are experts at knowing when to wait and when to pounce. This foxy canine reminds us to be patient, use camouflage when necessary, and rely on common sense to remain safe.

Are you game to expand your outlook and perceive beyond the ordinary? In legend, Fox is a shape-shifter and an uncommon guide to different worlds. Follow Fox to explore unique pathways and new ways of being. Slip between realms with Fox to encounter nature spirits and subtle dimensions. Astute and accomplished, Fox can help us to integrate magic with wisdom.

QUESTIONS

Feeling foxy? Maybe it's time to activate your adventurous spirit. Are you ready to start something new or explore an unusual idea? Fox encourages original perspectives and innovative expressions. Are you utilizing all of your abilities, considering all angles, sensing the right timing for action, and trusting your intuition? Seize opportunity, says Fox. Share your unique talents with the world!

GOAT

KEYS

- Light-footed
- Loves to climb
- Advocates a firm foundation
- Celebrates curiosity and adventure

TEACHING

Quick and agile, with a strong sense of stability, goats love to climb and jump. Mountain goats are especially good at traversing craggy cliffs and leaping across ledges. Goats sense natural energies and know how to move strategically, in ways that flow with the contours of nature, even when the terrain seems impossible to traverse.

Sure-footed and practical too, goats like to trek and explore, seeking out new vistas and different perspectives. Spirit of Goat prods us to roam around, appreciate what we find, and to engage life with all our senses. Goat helps us to move forward with patience and determination—without getting stuck. Goat knows the importance of a firm foundation even as we seek new heights of awareness.

Always curious, never bored, goats can make us laugh with their antics. Ever adventurous, Goat stimulates feelings of excitement, encouraging us to climb higher, see farther, and investigate different points of view. To do so is to experience the joy that Goat knows.

QUESTIONS

Feeling stuck? Backed into a corner? Unsure what to do next? Call upon Goat for some expert advice on how to maneuver safely while considering your options. You may be instructed to look around—carefully—in order to determine your next move. Goat can help you find your own path with clarity and confidence. In some cases, you may need to leap. But don't worry—with Goat, you will succeed.

MONKEY

KEYS
○—▸ Playful and creative
○—▸ Good communicator and thinker
○—▸ Knows how to weigh options

TEACHING
Lighthearted, with quick minds and nimble bodies, monkeys like to have fun. They are good communicators, using sounds, hand and body movements, facial expressions, as well as acrobatics and grooming, to exchange feelings and information. Some cultures believe monkeys converse with nature spirits, fairies, and other worldly beings. Spirit of Monkey can help us communicate with honesty and sensitivity.

Highly curious, monkeys like to explore. Playful and easygoing, they are also good thinkers and problem solvers. Monkey encourages us to open our minds, investigate our options, and imagine outcomes before making a decision. Monkey inspires creative thought and practical insight.

With long tails that grasp firmly, monkeys swing from branch to branch, assessing their next moves accurately. Intelligent, with good dexterity and adaptability, Monkey can help us progress through thinking tasks with similarly swift and graceful moves. Monkey knows that life can be both fun and educational.

QUESTIONS
Do you recall the old saying, "monkey see, monkey do"? It refers to imitation without understanding—a negative connotation since humans don't understand life as monkeys do. Lively and inventive, Monkey teaches through activity. Whether swinging from a tree or examining a leaf, young monkeys learn by doing. By engaging in Monkey's free-spirited play, you too may begin to soak up some of Monkey's common-sense knowledge. Are you ready for fun? Monkey knows there is wisdom in play.

MOUSE

KEYS

○→ Small but powerful
○→ Excellent attention to detail
○→ Skilled at finding secrets

TEACHING

Though Mouse is small, its teaching is powerful. Quick, smart, and lively, mice investigate life with thorough attentiveness. Alert to danger, they know how to avoid obstacles and hide in small spaces to observe safely. Curious and resourceful, mice like to explore and make use of what's available to feed, shelter, and comfort themselves. Mouse is adaptable.

Mouse teaches us to notice the little things. Check the fine print of contracts, investigate all nooks, cracks, and crevices before buying a house. Mouse knows that attentiveness to the small can help you later, when larger consequences may arise. Mouse can also help us to find secrets, to discover what is hidden or tucked away in small spaces. Mouse helps us pay attention to details and do one thing at a time so we can achieve great things.

Cute and gentle, Mouse is a good guide for children, helping them to feel safe and secure, and to hide when necessary. Mouse understands and embodies the power of the small.

QUESTIONS

Is your inner House of Mouse balanced and in order? While Mouse's energy can be of great assistance when focusing attention on detail, it can sometimes overwhelm. Too much and you may end up overanalyzing, nitpicking, or fixating on every little thing. Sound familiar? If so, remember that Mouse is adaptable. Tame obsessive scrutinization with a little play or rest. Mouse will accommodate.

PIG

KEYS
- ⊶ Intelligent
- ⊶ Resourceful
- ⊶ Playful and loving
- ⊶ Accepting

TEACHING

Humans see pigs in different ways—sloppy, greedy, and dirty or linked with good luck, wealth, strength, and sincerity. Spend some time with Pig and you'll see: pigs are good-natured, down to earth, and champions of common sense.

Mother pigs are protective and devoted, gently teaching young piglets through play and physical closeness. Pigs are satisfied with who they are and accepting of others. Their teaching is the same. Pig is compassionate and wants us to find our true self. Pig encourages us to express who we are and how we feel, and extend that courtesy to others.

Pigs are good foragers, using their sensitive snouts to root through leaves or soil for food. They like to explore and are creative in knowing what to do with what they find. Pig knows the value of digging beneath the surface to uncover what we need. Pig inspires self-knowledge and encourages us to find our own buried treasure within.

QUESTIONS

How do you feel about pigs? Think of five adjectives to describe pigs and then ask yourself: "How does this apply to me?" Pig prods us to look beneath the surface and uncover the truth beneath our many projections. If you're not a fan of pigs, you may want to rearrange your point of view. Pig offers deep wisdom with a playful snort. Have a mud bath, smell the earth, and lounge in the sunshine to celebrate your inner Pig.

PORCUPINE

KEYS

- Advocates peace
- Defends when necessary
- Lives a quiet, balanced life

TEACHING

Generally calm and good-natured, porcupines know how to take it easy. Roaming alone at night, they explore their surroundings at an unhurried pace. With finely tuned senses, they know when others are near, but rarely interact. Porcupine minds its own business and wishes everyone else would too.

With over 30,000 sharply pointed quills emanating from their body, porcupines know how to defend. Their quills are long, hollow hairs with barbed tips; when slapped into the skin of those who venture too close, they stick and embed. Porcupine is not afraid to protect itself when threatened, and advises us to do the same.

Mostly content and peaceful, however, Porcupine reassures us that life need not be problematic if our attitude is right. Porcupines live simply and quietly, either alone or with their pups. Young porcupines learn patience, observation, and the value of right living. Proponent of peaceful existence, Porcupine is a fan of live and let live.

QUESTIONS

Porcupine may show up to make a point. Are your words sharp, your actions stinging? Are you being too prickly? Or, perhaps you need to assert yourself and make your views stick? Either way, Porcupine can help you find balance within. Beneath their spiky appearance, porcupines are happy and secure. They follow their passions, rarely worry what others think, yet make their viewpoints known. Porcupine challenges you to express yourself confidently and respectfully, and allow others to do the same.

PRAIRIE DOG

KEYS

- Devoted to family
- Excellent communicators
- Love to collaborate
- Good problem solvers

TEACHING

Outgoing, friendly, and sociable, prairie dogs love togetherness! Sleeping in groups, touching noses and embracing, they live in close family units. Communities are sprawling underground labyrinths of interconnected tunnels and chambers, some housing millions of prairie dog residents.

Fast moving with rapid reflexes, prairie dogs promptly alert their group to danger. Naturally curious and quick-minded, they know how to solve problems and work together for the common good. Highly organized and efficient, prairie dogs also love to play and have fun. An excellent team player, Prairie Dog teaches love of family and group cooperation for comfortable living.

Prairie dogs are talented communicators, using a sophisticated system of unique barks and calls as well as gestures and movements. Prairie Dog can help us streamline communication and speak in concise, effective ways.

Living mostly underground, prairie dogs often pop up from burrow holes to survey their surroundings. Prairie Dog links aboveground viewpoints with underground feelings and emotions. Prairie Dog encourages us to be aware of that which is not seen yet resides just below the surface of awareness.

QUESTIONS

Is your life all work and no play? Or perhaps the reverse is true? Prairie Dog can offer some good advice on how to balance efficiency with fun, accomplishment with enjoyment. Take a tour of Prairie Dog's town to witness impressive industriousness fueled by group recreation. Prairie Dog stimulates both good work ethics and merriment.

RAM

KEYS
o—⊸ Determined
o—⊸ Confident
o—⊸ Powerful ruler
o—⊸ Initiates new beginnings

TEACHING

Rams are male bighorn sheep. With long fur and impressively large, curved horns, they settle disputes and dominance by crashing heads. Ram knows what it wants and how to get it. Its confidence is strong.

While female bighorns live peacefully with their young in communal groups, rams live in small herds and fight to determine leadership. Masterful, powerful, self-assured, Ram is an authority figure not easily deceived. Its big horns signify strong abilities to think and rule clearly. Ram invokes inner fortitude and helps us to express ourselves in assertive, practical ways.

Sure-footed and bold, rams can jump far and travel swiftly up steep mountain cliffs. Ram knows its abilities and understands its path. Encouraging us to do our best, Ram helps us to learn from our mistakes and gain wisdom through experience.

A powerful, creative force for growth, Ram initiates new beginnings. Ram advises a solid foundation to build assurance and strengthen self-esteem—this is how to express authority in a centered, grounded manner. Ram helps us to be strong.

QUESTIONS

Has Ram shown up in your life? If so, a new beginning may be imminent. Ram will encourage you to leap when the time is right. But you must know yourself and be fully present—otherwise, forget it. Ram offers the sensible, practical advice to draw upon the wisdom of the Earth as well as your own foundational core. Follow Ram's sage guidance and you will succeed.

RABBIT

KEYS
o—x Good luck
o—x Quick and observant
o—x Inspires appreciation of magic

TEACHING

Rabbit is lucky. Associated with longevity, happiness, fertility, and abundance, Rabbit is sometimes portrayed as a trickster and messenger to the moon. Also linked with fairies and nature spirits, Rabbit is a clever guide who knows how to move between worlds and enter other dimensional realities.

Quick and nimble, with strong reflexes, rabbits are sensitive to their environment. They can run fast and know how to hide. Rabbits may move suddenly to seize opportunity or freeze their motions when danger is near. Rabbit teaches us to observe carefully and react appropriately. Rabbit can help us face our fears, take intuitive leaps, and discover hidden openings that lead to deeper understanding.

Rabbits gestate quickly and propagate abundantly. There is a magic to their multiplication as well as their ability to disappear into holes or pop up unexpectedly—such as from a magician's hat. Quiet and unassuming, Rabbit helps us to notice magic in the world.

QUESTIONS

Are you hiding something? Is it a secret you are keeping from others—or from yourself? Rabbit can help you to peer through self-deception so that you may live more honestly. Rabbit knows how to find the dark, forgotten pieces of self that are hidden in the subconscious. Rabbit inspires us to invite those lost selves up into the light—to unburden ourselves from secrecy and judgment. With Rabbit, we can learn to become lighter and more joyfully whole.

RACCOON

KEYS

- Curious and intelligent
- Inspires creativity
- Likes to have fun
- Celebrates wonder

TEACHING

Clever and curious, raccoons love to investigate. With dextrous paws and an inquisitive mind, they like to turn over, open, unlock, and manipulate objects to discover how they work. Raccoons are resourceful and inventive at using what they find. Raccoon encourages us to be creative in repurposing items in new and different ways. Raccoon advocates the joy and fun of recycling!

Mostly nocturnal, raccoons can see in the dark and love to explore when humans are sleeping. Wearing their trademark black bandit mask, raccoons will readily plunder trash cans and make themselves at home in cellars or attics. Fun-loving yet mischievous, raccoons have a reputation for nuisance.

Finely attuned to their environment with good observational skills, raccoons are quick-witted and adapt easily to new situations. Easygoing and easily fascinated, they are captivated by almost anything—shiny objects, holes in trees, rushing water. Raccoon reminds us that there is wonder in the world.

QUESTIONS

Up for a little adventure? Even if you don't have a specific problem or need, Raccoon is a teacher that never fails to engage and inspire. Roam with Raccoon for an array of experiences: smell the warm earth, play in the glistening rain, follow paths to uncover secrets, or enjoy a harmless prank. Raccoon can help you loosen up, have some fun, and appreciate the simple joys that are all around you.

SKUNK

KEYS

- Protection
- Peace
- Self-respect

TEACHING

Well known for the spray of their distinct odor, skunks use their pungent message not to injure, but to defend. Skunks are placid and partial to peace. When need be, however, their relatively harmless—yet extremely effective—scent communicates clearly: please stay away!

Skunks are humble and unassuming. They will stand their ground, but prefer to be left alone. Tranquil, silent, and self-assured, Skunk can help us to soothe and settle, and move forward with peace. As a gentle guide to serenity, Skunk works well with children, especially those that are easily excitable. Skunk comforts and reminds us that all is well.

Skunk knows the value of passive strength. Its bold white stripes symbolize clarity and composure. Skunk teaches that the way to gain confidence is not by showing off, but by being who we are.

Skunk encourages us to express ourselves truthfully and behave calmly. Skunk teaches us to avoid conflict by respecting ourselves and others.

QUESTIONS

Are you prone to heated arguments? Do you respond loudly to the slightest provocation? Take it easy, says Skunk. What are you afraid of? Most animals leave Skunk alone because its odoriferous reputation is well known. You may not need to create a big stink to express yourself or display your power. Skunk can help you to be assertive without bullying or shouting. Take a walk with Skunk and learn to meet life's challenges with calm assurance.

SQUIRREL

KEYS

- ○—ᴛ Friendly
- ○—ᴛ Good communicator
- ○—ᴛ Plans for the future
- ○—ᴛ Teaches us to be prepared

TEACHING

Cute and frisky, with big bushy tails, squirrels are playful yet always have a plan. Squirrels are agile—scampering up trees, leaping across branches—and like to have fun. They will change direction abruptly, however, to evade danger. Squirrel teaches us to act quickly and avoid peril by being alert and thinking fast.

Squirrels gather nuts and seeds in fall, storing them away in private hiding spots. Alert to opportunity with good planning skills, squirrels stockpile resources for lean winter months. Spirit of Squirrel models the importance of saving and preparing for the future. Because squirrels don't recover all they hide, they tuck away extra supplies. Squirrel teaches that even good plans aren't guaranteed, so it's wise to have a backup.

Squirrels are outgoing and sociable, whether chattering amiably or calling loudly to warn of danger. Squirrel reminds us to value friendly conversation and watch out for others. Friendly and resourceful, Squirrel teaches us to balance our energies and be fully involved in all we do—taking time to socialize and play as well as preparing for our future.

QUESTIONS

Have you squirreled away the basics? Do you have enough cash, food, and supplies to cover bases in an emergency? Squirrel knows the value of planning for the future. Get organized and focus on the details to determine exactly what you need, not only to survive but to thrive. With Squirrel you will be well prepared.

WOLVERINE

Generally solitary, wolverines require a large area to roam. Proud and fierce, they rarely back down, even from much larger animals. Wolverines intimidate with their ferocity, but it's not a bluff—they may hunt and kill animals several times their size. Hardy and self-sufficient, wolverines know how to take care of themselves.

Wolverines are adaptable and incredibly determined. They will trek through extreme weather for food, and do all they can to survive. Spirit of Wolverine teaches us to overcome adversity not just with perseverance but with a kind of wild joy. Wolverine loves a challenge almost as much as it loves succeeding.

KEYS

○—⚓ Intimidating
○—⚓ Fierce
○—⚓ Loves a challenge
○—⚓ Won't back down

TEACHING

Wild and unpredictable is Wolverine, the largest member of the weasel family. Stocky and muscular, with powerful jaws and sharp claws, wolverines are very strong and very resolute. Though small in stature, they are powerfully built— even their short legs are robust enough to move through deep snow. Wolverines possess condensed energy and spring into action quickly.

Wolverines can be ferocious and won't let go once they have focused on what they want. Wolverine is a true warrior that exudes strength, resilience, and power.

QUESTIONS

Do you need to fight—for justice, for love, for survival? When desperate times require desperate measures, call on Wolverine for staying power to achieve. With Wolverine beside you, you will not let go and you will not back down. Wolverine will help you give it your all.

BIRDS

KEYS

- Mental clarity
- The thrill of flight
- Expansive perspectives
- Higher knowledge
- Connection to spirit

BLUE JAY

KEYS

- Sees clearly
- Speaks assertively
- Teaches us to be smart and bold

TEACHING

With its bright eyes and dazzling blue feathers accented in black and white, Blue Jay symbolizes clarity, balance, and connection to spirit. In Native American mythology, jays are signs of seeing clearly and speaking truthfully. Their blue coloring is reminiscent of a brilliant sky and corresponds to the sixth chakra, summoning intuition and perception. Blue Jay helps us to see what we know to be true.

Members of the crow family, blue jays are intelligent and self-aware. They have a wide range of vocalizations and can mimic other birds as well as humans. Jays can be quite loud at times. Spirit of Blue Jay teaches us to use our voice creatively and assertively.

Sometimes bold and sassy, jays will steal food and nesting materials from others. Fearless when protecting themselves or their young, blue jays will not easily back down. They may team up with other jays to fend off stronger birds of prey. Resourceful and clever, blue jays know how to take advantage of a situation. Study with Blue Jay and you'll learn not only how to play the game but how to win.

QUESTIONS

Is there something you're not wanting to see? Jay sometimes calls us to attention when we're not being totally honest or forthright with ourselves. With its penetrating gaze, Blue Jay prods us to take a clear, deep look within. Jay offers you the chance to see the truth and act accordingly.

CHICKEN

KEYS
- Intelligent and brave
- Connected to the Earth
- Senses subtle energies
- Celebrates diversity

TEACHING
One of the few birds that don't fly, Chicken doesn't seem to mind. Socially minded and keenly observant, chickens like to gather together and scratch the earth to find food. They are inquisitive and skilled at finding what they need. Spirit of Chicken teaches practical wisdom by inspiring curiosity and reminding us to stay grounded and pay attention in order to unearth our needs.

Cautious and alert, chickens are quick to notice danger and sensitive to subtle energies. Chicken can help us to be more watchful and aware, and to be more empathic with others.

Though they enjoy living in groups, chickens celebrate individuality and variety. There are many different types of chickens with a wide range of feather pattern and color—black, brown, and white to bright red, yellow, and blue. Some chickens have crests and crowns, others fleshy neck lobes called wattles. Chicken encourages us to be creative and express our uniquely individual nature. Chicken has a strong spirit and urges us to be stronger too.

QUESTIONS
Are you a bit cowardly? Do others call you "chicken"? Would you be surprised to know that in many cultures chickens symbolize courage? Perhaps it is because they have a proud, inner strength and can be aggressive when defending. Call on Chicken to ruffle up your feathers. Learn to express the full power of your unique self without apology. Chicken can help you succeed.

DOVE/PIGEON

KEYS
o—⚡ Gentle nature
o—⚡ Nurturing and protective
o—⚡ Symbolizes love and peace
o—⚡ Spiritual messenger

TEACHING

Doves and pigeons belong to the same family, and their names are used somewhat interchangeably. There are over 300 species of pigeons and doves. Incredibly adaptable, they live almost everywhere—in the city and the country, in forests and woodlands, on sandy deserts and islands.

Unlike most birds, doves and pigeons produce a special type of milk to feed their chicks. What's more, both males and females produce this milk and share in the responsibility of caring for their young. Spirit of Dove is a symbol of nurturing, family love, and togetherness.

The cooing sound of doves is soft and soothing. Dove is a good protective guide for children, helping them to feel safe and well loved. Doves sing throughout the day but especially during early morning and evening hours—transitional times when the veils between the Earth and spirit worlds are thin. In religious art, doves are a symbol of grace, purity, and the presence of spirit. Dove is a spiritual messenger, opening the heart and awakening higher love. Dove steers us gently into alignment with our soul's purpose.

QUESTIONS

Are you troubled, worried, or overcome by unhappy thoughts that won't let go? Appeal to Dove for some stillness and serenity. Dove's calming presence and gentle manner can help you to release all that is painful, traumatic, or upsetting. Breathe deep. Dove is a promise that peace is near.

EAGLE

KEYS

- Powerful teacher
- Knows what it wants
- Communicates with spirit
- Helps us to express our true self

TEACHING

A strong bird with powerful wings, Eagle's actions are swift and focused. Whether soaring at high altitudes for long distances or diving faster than a speeding car, eagles know how to harness nature's energy to move efficiently and effectively. Eagle helps us to transcend limiting viewpoints and open ourselves to greater vistas of awareness.

Eagles have excellent vision and are keenly aware of their environment. Even from high perspectives, they can spot a rabbit up to two miles away. With strong talons and a sharp beak, eagles direct their movements and take what they need. Eagle knows when to see the big picture and when to zoom in on important details.

Eagle also sees through deception and is thus associated with truth and justice. In the Native American tradition, eagles are messenger birds that carry prayers to the spirit world and bring us visions in return. Eagle awakens intuitive insights and deepens spiritual understanding, allowing us to journey far yet still remain grounded on the earth.

QUESTIONS

Do you want to elevate your awareness, fine-tune your skills of perception, or enhance creativity? Eagle can help you become stronger, clearer, more accurate, and more innovative. Eagle encourages us to dream big, hone our innate abilities, and open ourselves up to greater possibilities. Fly with Eagle to break free from self-imposed limitations. Are you ready to soar and rise above?

FLAMINGO

KEYS

- Beauty
- Grace
- Balance
- Nourishment

TEACHING

With tall thin legs, hearty oblong bodies, and elegantly curved necks, flamingos are a study in equilibrium. Whether standing upon one leg, wading through deep water, or flying in dazzling formations with their flock, flamingos are fluid and graceful. Flamingo is a teacher of balance in all arenas—be it physical, emotional, or spiritual.

Flamingo's bright pink and white feathers evoke beauty and the inner warmth of happiness. Flamingo is not a show-off, but not afraid to express its bright, impressive colors either. Flamingo teaches us to be who we are, to shine our natural beauty, and love ourselves wholeheartedly.

Flamingos mate for life. Highly social, they live closely together, sometimes in groups numbering tens of thousands. Caring and devoted, flamingos are loyal to their flock but never lose their sense of self. They fly in tight formation in a distinctive style—with outstretched necks in front and straightened legs behind.

Spirit of Flamingo is a good guide for those who journey, whether physically or spiritually.

QUESTIONS

Flamingos get their pink coloring from what they eat; if they don't get enough nutrients, they will pale in color. What's your color like lately? Are you nourishing your deep self, doing what you want, and living your heart's desire? If the answer is no, Flamingo can help you find the sustenance required to come back into healthy balance. Flock with Flamingo to nurture deeper needs and express your soul creatively.

GOOSE

KEYS
- ○—→ Strong and caring
- ○—→ Loyal to their flock
- ○—→ Extremely protective

TEACHING

A sacred bird to ancient peoples, geese have lived on this planet for over 12 million years. Connected with the north wind and change, Goose is a symbol of fertility, fidelity, and loyalty.

Strong and confident, geese are good navigators, communicators, and cooperative team players. Flying in streamlined V-formations, they take turns navigating and work well together to watch for danger and good places to land. A supportive guide for long distance travel, Goose reminds us to respect personal rhythms and allow others to help when we are tired.

Caring and compassionate, geese are sensitive to flock members, especially those needing assistance. If one goose is injured, another will stay until it recovers. Strongly loyal, with deep bonds of affection, geese do not allow other geese to be alone when sick or dying.

Geese are faithful and mate for life. Extremely territorial and protective of young goslings, they will honk loudly, charge, and flap their wings dramatically if threatened or disturbed. Call on Goose to intimidate strangers who come too close.

QUESTIONS

Are you a leader or a follower? More to the point, do you think it must be one way or the other? Goose teaches that leadership can be shared. Goose knows the value of teamwork and sharing talents for the good of the whole. Take wing with Goose to pursue your goals in efficient ways that succeed with the helpful support of others.

GULL

KEYS

○━┑ Bold and daring

○━┑ Alert to opportunity

○━┑ Inspires personal freedom

TEACHING

Gull is a general name for a variety of medium-sized seabirds, usually white or gray, sometimes with black markings on their wings or head. Not all gulls live near the sea, though most live and breed near water.

Bold opportunists, gulls like to scavenge. Though they know how to hunt for fish and crabs, gulls prefer to forage shorelines, steal food from others, or call on tourists for crumbs. Alert and adaptable, they are good at seizing an opportunity—brazenly picking through trash and landfills for discarded yet tasty morsels. Spirit of Gull teaches us not to take things for granted, but rather to take advantage of circumstance and make the most of it.

Loud and squawky, gulls call out for what they need when they need it. Gull teaches us to use our voice, make our desires known, and speak loudly when necessary. Strong and daring flyers, gulls are sometimes associated with freedom and unconventional spiritual pursuits. Gull encourages us to break free from societal expectations, to fly high, follow our dreams, and live up to our soul's potential. Gull helps us soar.

QUESTIONS

Are you worried about what others think? Are you allowing their judgments to keep you small? Forget about that! squawks Gull. Though they may seem common to humans, gulls don't care what humans think. Bold and brash and unashamed, Gull helps us to let go of superficial judgments and reclaim our true selves. Gull helps us to be real.

HAWK

KEYS
- Powerful bird of prey
- Intelligent and perceptive
- Fine-tunes awareness

TEACHING

With their piercing gaze, impressive wingspan, and exceptionally sharp claws, hawks mean business. Determined, focused, powerful raptors, they fly fast and react quickly. Spirit of Hawk teaches us to be strong and decisive, to see clearly and move with purpose, to direct our actions with no wasted time or effort.

In the ancient world, hawks announced the death of leaders, helped warriors in battle, and assisted newly departed souls to enter the spirit realm. Associated with many gods and goddesses, Hawk provided sage council and fierce protection. Hawk links humans with the divine and teaches respect.

Extremely intelligent, with keen eyesight, hawks perceive clearly and are good problem solvers. They know how to adapt in creative ways. Hawk awakens inner vision, helping us to see our talents and use them in the best ways possible.

A symbol of insight and finely tuned awareness, Hawk helps us sharpen our perception, enhance our intuition, and develop visionary abilities. Some say you cannot choose Hawk to be your guide. Rather, Hawk chooses you.

QUESTIONS

Has Hawk been circling your awareness lately? If so, pay attention—especially to what you may be overlooking. Hawk's presence is often a sign to look deeply inside yourself. Are you headed in the right direction? What is it you really need to see? Hawk stirs deep awareness, recommending the release of all diversions so that you may focus fully in the present.

HUMMINGBIRD

KEYS

- Fast, talented flyer
- Inspires wonder
- Spreads happiness and joy

TEACHING

As the smallest of birds and the only one that can fly backwards, Hummingbird is unique. Flying sideways and upside down, hovering in midair, hummingbirds flash their vibrant, iridescent feathers. Hummingbird is a special spirit that inspires us to appreciate beauty and the magical wonders of life.

Fast and agile, hummingbirds beat their wings so quickly it creates an audible hum—sometimes linked to healing.

Visiting hundreds of flowers a day, hummingbirds expend enormous energy. At night their metabolism plummets. Cold and motionless throughout dark hours, hummingbirds reanimate to the warmth of the rising sun, and are thus linked to revitalization and resurrection.

Despite their delicate appearance, hummingbirds are bold and sometimes aggressive. They will fend off larger birds by using their long beaks as weapons. Honored as a warrior in some cultures, Hummingbird encourages bravery. Symbol of beauty, love, and honor, Hummingbird teaches us to sense deeply and find the good in all.

QUESTIONS

Need a little inspiration in your life? Close your eyes and think of Hummingbird. Sometimes called the flying jewel or flower bird, Hummingbird awakens joy, awe, and wonder. Spend time with Hummingbird to recognize the brilliant talents and beauty that reside within you—yes, you! How could you have missed it? Tiny yet powerful, Hummingbird sees radiance everywhere, and knows that we are all a part of it. Hummingbird invites you to open your eyes and shine.

OSTRICH

KEYS

- Biggest living bird
- Grounds wisdom
- Advocates self-awareness

TEACHING

The tallest and largest of birds, Ostrich has wings but cannot fly—its body is simply too heavy. However, Ostrich can run—very quickly, almost as if flying upon the earth. Ostrich helps ground avian energies of flight and soaring spirit in balanced, earth-based ways.

Once known as the "camel bird," ostriches have long legs, necks, and eyelashes, and— like camels—can go days without water. Spirit of Ostrich teaches us to stand tall and persevere.

Contrary to popular belief, ostriches don't really bury their heads in the sand. They do, however, bury their enormous eggs in shallow holes in the ground. Several times a day females lower their heads to gently turn the eggs. The human belief that ostriches are attempting to hide or avoid reality is misguided at best. Ostrich's teaching is quite the opposite: to be responsible for our creations and aware of all our actions. Ostrich encourages us to recognize self-deception and accept the truths we need to see.

QUESTIONS

Attracting too much attention lately? Want to be less visible but have nowhere to go? Ostrich has a plan. To avoid detection from predators, ostriches lie with their head and neck flat on the ground so that from a distance they appear to be a large mound of earth. It's fitting that the largest of birds offers you advice on how to hide in plain sight, for such is the irony and allure of Ostrich.

OWL

KEYS

- ⚷ Sees in the dark
- ⚷ Pierces illusion
- ⚷ Lights the way to inner wisdom

TEACHING

Silent and stealthy, owls are traditionally known as birds of mystery. Linked with Athena, goddess of wisdom, as well as the moon, the night, and the feminine, Owl awakens inner vision. Guardian to the underworld, Owl heralds prophecy and secret knowledge.

Nocturnal hunters with excellent senses, owls have keen night vision and navigate well through dense forests. Owl teaches us to survey our surroundings carefully so that we can act quickly, with precision. Owl sees through deception and illusion, encouraging us to move beyond the fears that hold us back. For those ready to penetrate the shadowy mysteries of life, Owl is a master guide to dream journeying and exploring astral realms.

Flying swiftly upon strong, soft wings, owls swoop quietly upon their prey. Owl knows secrets of the night and can help us move unnoticed in the dark, with clarity and composure. Owl teaches us to pay attention and learn, for this is how we acquire wisdom. This is how we become a wise old owl.

QUESTIONS

Are you afraid of the dark? Do you want to know why? Ask Owl to shed some light on this mystery. Owl knows how to clear away that which no longer serves—limiting beliefs, repressed emotions, unwarranted fears—in order to discover hidden truths. Owl guides you to see clearly so that you may discover your own wisdom within.

PARROT

KEYS

○━ Excellent communicator
○━ Bright, bold, joyful
○━ Inspires creativity

TEACHING

With their bright, vivid feathers, bold, joyous manner, and loud, boisterous calls, parrots aren't afraid to have fun. Friendly and sociable, they live in large, lively flocks. There are almost 400 species of parrot throughout the world; most are brilliantly colored and all are extremely intelligent.

Despite a lack of vocal cords, parrots are well known for their communication skills, and can imitate a range of sounds, including human voices. Spirit of Parrot is an excellent guide to learning new forms of communication, such as a foreign language, sign language, or the symbolic language of dreams.

Occasionally raucous, Parrot encourages us to lighten up and enjoy ourselves. But the reverse is also part of Parrot's teaching—to be sensitive and diplomatic, to choose our words carefully, to be aware of what we are saying and how we are saying it. Parrot links humans with the bird kingdom and bridges understanding between species. Parrot motivates us to connect and find harmony with others.

QUESTIONS

Did you know that finding a parrot feather is a sign of creative encouragement from the spirit world? If feeling ordinary and uninspired, have a look around. Parrot reminds you to stay alert to opportunity, recognize hints from nature (such as fallen feathers), follow inner hunches, and celebrate the unconventional. You need not find a feather to be inspired. Rather, call on Parrot for new ideas, creative insights, and innovation.

PEACOCK

The iridescent blue-green "eyes" on peacock feathers represent wisdom and spiritual insight. When male peacocks display their tail feathers, we see a profusion of brilliant eyes. All-seeing Peacock awakens clairvoyant abilities, helping us to see into the past as well as the future in order to better understand our present.

Advocating wholeness and confidence, Peacock urges us to reclaim the parts of ourselves that we have judged ugly or unworthy. Helping us to love all of ourselves, Peacock reminds that beauty is first found within. A bird of personal empowerment, Peacock encourages us to reveal our true colors and shine.

KEYS

o—⇁ Enjoys life
o—⇁ Advocates pleasure
o—⇁ Champions self-esteem
o—⇁ Inspires brilliance

TEACHING

Living in the same place for most of their lives, peacocks are birds of habit. Homebodies as well as hedonists, they are playful and relish pleasure, and find nothing wrong with that. Peacock laughs at judgment and teaches appreciation for what we have. Peacock nudges us to be at home with ourselves, to love who we are, and to enjoy our lives fully.

QUESTIONS

Feeling blah? Have your life colors faded to monochromatic black and white? Perhaps you need a flash of technicolored brilliance, courtesy of Peacock. Learn to strut your stuff and bring back the radiance of your being. Peacock's influence can help you shine brighter, resonate deeper, and vibrate with vitality. Reenergize your spirit, display your beauty, and celebrate happiness—that's the way to be proud as a peacock.

PELICAN

KEYS

○—ᴛ Works well with others

○—ᴛ Blends air and water teachings

○—ᴛ Scoops up what it needs

TEACHING

Pelicans are team players. They hunt cooperatively and nest together in large colonies. Gregarious and friendly, they accept help from others and offer assistance when needed. Altruistic and attentive, Pelican encourages us to share and recognize the value of group efforts.

Large birds with long bills and a handy neck pouch, pelicans are buoyant and adaptable. Comfortable both in air and water, they are strong swimmers, yet also love to glide high upon thermal currents. Pelicans plummet from the sky and dive deep into the water or skim the surface to scoop up fish. Joining elevated perceptions with proficiency in the fluid world of emotions, Pelican can help us be more comfortable with our feelings and understand them more clearly.

Soaring gracefully, moving with precision and control, pelicans are excellent long-distance travelers. Pelican is a good companion for lengthy expeditions or shared journeys with others. Pelican can help us adapt with a calm and contemplative mind.

QUESTIONS

Have you been searching for this or that, not really finding what you need? Take a hint from Pelican. Stop rushing around and position yourself advantageously so that what you want comes to you. Smart and alert, Pelican finds a favorable perch and waits for what it wants. Be patient and look carefully. Then, when the time is right, invoke Pelican to help you expertly scoop up what you need.

PENGUIN

KEYS

- Flies through water
- Connects realms
- Integrates opposites
- Encourages good manners

TEACHING

Penguins fly—but not through the air. Rather, they use their wings to glide underwater. Penguins are graceful, masterful swimmers and can leap impressively between land and sea. Though more at home in water, penguins also move upon frozen land and icebergs with agility and ease. Penguin can help us better understand our emotional realm in a grounded way.

Penguin enhances fluidity of movement in dream realms. Skilled in lucid dreaming and astral travel, Penguin knows how to recall and integrate messages from other dimensions into conscious awareness. Penguin advocates adaptability, encouraging us to stay flexible, observant, and aware. Penguin can help us to slide between realities in order to explore and learn more about ourselves.

Penguins use ritualized gestures such as bowing to each other as a sign of greeting to maintain strong social bonds. Penguins respect good manners and depend upon proper etiquette to keep their big colonies healthy and happy.

QUESTIONS

Are you playful or proper? Penguin asks, why not be both? Stylishly dressed in black and white, penguins appear formal in their trademark tuxedos, yet waddle on land in cute, humorous ways. Both males and females warm their eggs and raise their young together. Penguin understands the art of balance and can help us integrate opposites—black and white, male and female, protocol and playfulness—in simple yet elegant ways.

RAVEN

KEYS
- Deepens awareness
- Connects worlds
- Assists in healing
- Helps us to change

TEACHING
Rich in mythology, Raven is a powerful bird that oversees changes in consciousness, helping us to deepen awareness and move between worlds. Sometimes known as the messenger bird, Raven brings information from the spirit realm to Earth. In Native American traditions, Raven is the great trickster. In Norse lore, two ravens (named Thought and Memory) tell the great god Odin all that is happening on Earth. Bad omen to some, keeper of secrets to others, Raven holds both magic and mystery.

Intelligent, sharp-witted, and good at mimicry, ravens have their own language and understand ours. Innovative and clever, they can solve problems quickly. Their loud calls—piercing at times—are auditory aids for shifting awareness. Known for its shape-shifting ability, Raven assists with spiritual initiations and awakenings of consciousness.

Raven aids healing by reminding us that we have the power to change ourselves and the course of our lives. Raven teaches discernment, self-knowledge, and the importance of introspection in knowing ourselves more wholly. Raven holds old wisdom and can connect us to the deeper mysteries of life and death.

QUESTIONS
Raven remembers a time when humans and animals communicated freely. Do you? Breathe deeply and close your eyes. Invite Raven to reawaken your skills in the Universal Language. A master guide to recalling all that we have forgotten, Raven helps us penetrate inner mysteries and recollect the hidden stories of who we really are.

ROBIN

KEYS
- ⚬— Inspires creativity
- ⚬— Initiates new growth
- ⚬— Encourages self-expression

TEACHING

Cheer up! Cheer up! Robin's happy song announces spring, growth, new beginnings, and creative opportunity. Robin urges us to move forward with our projects by trying new things. Experiment, innovate, and say "yes" to what presents itself in order to expand awareness and heighten creativity. A symbol of enthusiasm, joy, and rejuvenation, Robin helps us find what we need and nourish ourselves so that we can generate change.

Robins sing both to communicate and claim territory. Males do not fight, but rather puff up their feathers and sing! Robin reminds us to sing our unique song and proudly claim what is ours. Encouraging us to give voice to the creative spirit within, Robin sings to cheer us up and cheer us on.

Robin's red breast symbolizes a warm heart and the coming day. In some myths, the sun rises and sets on Robin's wings. Robin's yellow beak is linked with sunshine—a reminder to be optimistic in our speech. Robin urges us to embrace our inner light: to see clearly, speak kindly, and act with integrity.

QUESTIONS

Do you hear Robin's call? If so, it's time to get moving, for a creative change is coming your way. Announcing significant shifts of consciousness and new beginnings, Robin can help you take advantage of this time period to move ahead rapidly and efficiently. Robin enthusiastically urges you to get started now! Be prepared to take wing and welcome your bright future.

STORK

Considered a good omen, Stork is a symbol of protection, longevity, and a happy family life.

Storks make large nests—up to six feet wide and eight feet deep—typically used for several years. Associated with safety and security, stork nests perched atop roofs or chimneys are believed to protect that household from fire and theft.

Though mute, Storks can be quite loud. They communicate by snapping their bills, creating a sharp clattering sound. Stork models how to express ourselves in unconventional ways and still be heard by others.

KEYS

⊶ Ushers in the new
⊶ Offers protection
⊶ Brings good luck

TEACHING

Legends that link storks with the arrival of babies are ancient. While the reality is quite different of course, the symbolism is fitting. Stork heralds action and new beginnings that link the physical and spiritual worlds. Stork brings innovative ideas, important plans, and significant adventures in which a greater understanding of spirit may unfold.

Large, heavy, and long-legged, storks have huge wingspans—some over ten feet wide. Storks make use of their wings, flapping them to scare off predators.

QUESTIONS

Are you expecting? Stork's arrival signals a special delivery of something new—a project, love interest, child, or opportunity. Stork offers clarity and a better understanding of how your path is about to unfold. Something notable is going to happen and it's time to move forward. Symbol of inspiration and luck, Stork can help you take appropriate action.

SWAN

KEYS

○⟶ Beauty

○⟶ Grace

○⟶ Strength

○⟶ Ferocity

TEACHING

Muse to poets, artists, and musicians, Swan inspires eloquence, grace, and beauty. In legends, swans sing so sweetly they cause humans to swoon with sleep. With their dazzling white feathers, long curved necks, and elegant movements, there is an ethereal quality to swans. Symbol of love, soul, devotion, and spiritual freedom, Swan's persona is one we have idealized for centuries.

The reality is that swans are very strong, very determined, and sometimes very fierce. Fast flyers, they beat their large wings steadily, with great endurance, to migrate at high altitudes over long distances. Incredibly territorial, they may aggressively break bones of those who disturb their territory. Poised and confident, Swan teaches us to draw upon our inner strength when needed. Swan can be a particularly powerful guide for those who appear small or fragile.

Associated with love because they mate for life and travel in pairs, Swan encourages commitment and devotion. Swan awakens inner beauty as well as strength, and reminds us to follow our path with honor and integrity.

QUESTIONS

Need some assistance combining thoughts with feelings, or expressing spiritual desires in practical ways? Swan moves masterfully through different realms—air, water, land—transitioning between them with style and assurance. Swan can help you to join and integrate interior realms so that you can better know and more seamlessly express the fullness of who you are. That, says Swan, is a powerful key to inner strength.

VULTURE

Vulture helps us to accept death as a natural part of life's grand cycle. In doing so, we may appreciate the fullness of our lives in more meaningful ways.

Smart, practical navigators, vultures use thermals in the air to follow easy routes of travel. Spirit of Vulture elevates our awareness, offers an expansive overview of life, and helps us to soar above limitations. Vultures do not hunt but seize what is available. Resourceful, clever, and a bit unconventional, Vulture reminds us to be perceptive as well as creative when regarding the resources around us. Patient and insightful, Vulture encourages us to go with the flow.

KEYS
o—⚷ Helpful recycler
o—⚷ Symbol of renewal
o—⚷ Offers unconventional wisdom

TEACHING

Efficient scavengers and excellent recyclers, vultures are nature's garbage collectors, providing the important— though often thankless—task of cleansing the earth. Vulture advocates that we all clean up our messes.

Some cultures employ "sky burials" in which the dead are offered to vultures for consumption. Named the "death eater" by the Mayans, Vulture was considered a powerful symbol of renewal, cleansing, and transformation.

QUESTIONS

Feeling stuck? Despondent? Disheartened and discouraged? Vulture wisely reminds you that the spirit works in mysterious ways. You may not understand the significance of the events or emotions occurring in this moment, but in time you will. Vulture urges you to trust and accept. No matter how difficult things are now, change will occur. It must, says Vulture, for that is the natural flow of life and death.

WOODPECKER

KEYS
○—⇥ Protective and assertive
○—⇥ Demands attention
○—⇥ Alerts us to opportunity

TEACHING

With the sharp rap-rap-rapping of their beaks, woodpeckers shake us awake and call us to attention. Using the chisel-like tips of their strong bills, woodpeckers drill holes in trees and expertly probe beneath the bark with their long sticky tongues, grabbing insects to devour. Spirit of Woodpecker can help us peck away at surface layers so that we may explore deeper layers of self and find the treasures hidden below.

Woodpeckers nest in hollow cavities of trees and cacti. When other birds attempt to usurp these highly coveted chambers, woodpeckers become quite aggressive. Woodpecker reminds us to protect our homes and be alert to intrusion.

Sometimes viewed as messengers to other worlds, woodpeckers use drumming—rapid pecks of varying rhythms—to communicate. Woodpecker's loud, persistent hammering alerts us to the power of sound. Respectful of the unconventional,

Woodpecker encourages us to be innovative and explore alternate forms of communication. Woodpecker supports us in finding our own path and rhythm.

QUESTIONS

Has Woodpecker been tapping your awareness lately? If so, a window of opportunity may be near. Is it time to renew an old project, finish a current one, or start something new? Pay attention and use your head—for Woodpecker reminds us to think before we act. Be alert to messages from nature and honor intuitive prompts. Work with Woodpecker to gain the focus and determination necessary to keep going and not give up.

INSECTS & ARACHNIDS

KEYS

⚷ Talented teachers of transformation

⚷ Adaptable

⚷ Self-reliant

⚷ Embody mystery

ANT

Extremely community-minded, ants look out for their fellow ants. Devoted to the colony, each ant performs its duties for the good of the whole. Ants honor social order by respecting individuals, helping each other, and joining together for common aims.

Tireless workers, ants are also good planners and architects, creating complex homes with numerous chambers and deep, sprawling tunnels that may connect with neighboring colonies. Ant encourages us to be the master architect of our life, and wisely reminds us that we may enhance our creation with the help of others.

KEYS

o—¬ Hardworking
o—¬ Patient
o—¬ Good architect
o—¬ Values team effort

TEACHING

With patience and persistence, ants hunt, gather, and create amazing anthills. Steadfast and tenacious, they will carry food and leaves several miles back to their colony. Ants do not advocate the quick or easy way, but rather, the best way. Good problem solvers, they know how to circumvent obstacles and achieve their goals. Ant teaches us to do things correctly, one step at a time, without giving up.

QUESTIONS

Feeling impatient? Things not happening quickly enough? Ant wonders if the problem is your perception of the situation. Sit beside an anthill and you may better understand that creation takes time. Don't get ahead of yourself. Ever patient Ant urges you to create a solid foundation in all you do and honor the natural process of growth. Step by step, Ant can help you manifest your dreams in ways that will benefit both you and the world.

BEE

KEYS

⊶ Inspires love

⊶ Offers healing

⊶ Invites us to taste the sweetness of life

TEACHING

Over 20,000 species of bees live worldwide in a diverse range of habitats. Representing wisdom, fertility, mystery, and joy, Bee oversees a good percentage of plant and human food pollination. As they collect nectar from flowers, bees pick up tiny pollen grains, which are later deposited in other flowers. Thus pollination occurs. Bee teaches the importance of both giving and receiving, reminding us to honor the natural cycle of exchange.

Bees dance to share the location of flowers, water, or new sites with other bees. Enthusiastic and creative, Bee reminds us that communication can be a moving art.

Keenly focused and finely attuned to their endeavors, bees are both busy and sensitive. The sound of their buzz may awaken spiritual insights, heighten our intuition, and help to heal. Their honey is also recognized as a healing agent and food for baby bees and humans. Bee is a symbol of spiritual wealth, health, nourishment, and the sweetness of life.

QUESTIONS

Bees were once believed to defy the laws of physics since their body is too large for their wings to allow flight. Scientists later discovered that their fast wing movements do allow them to fly—something Bee has known all along. Is it time for you to break free of limited constraints and take flight? Bee encourages you to fly in the face of convention and follow your dreams. Release small-minded views and soar with Bee!

BEETLE

KEYS
- Diversity
- Abundance
- Renewal
- Change

TEACHING

Residents of planet Earth for over 300 million years, beetles now make up 40 percent of all known insects. Some drab, some dotted, some brilliant as gemstones, the over 380,000 species of beetles come in a wide variety of colors, shapes, and sizes. Symbol of change, adaptation, and innovation, Beetle is impressively abundant, incredibly diverse, and continues to evolve.

Masters of metamorphosis, beetles transform their bodies from eggs and grubs to winged insects. With hard yet lightweight forewings that sheath flight wings below, Beetle knows how to protect the delicate. Beetle can help us to feel safe even as our awareness soars.

Revered as a sacred symbol of resurrection, the scarab beetle was worn for protection in ancient Egypt and placed with mummies to ensure continued life in the afterlife. Beetle safeguards knowledge, both of the past and future, and is an enigmatic guide to immortality. Symbolizing omens and death, good luck and happiness, renewal of life and vitality, beetles continue to confound, amaze, and inspire.

QUESTIONS

Feeling powerless in face of the world's immensity? As if no matter what you do, nothing will change? The rhinoceros beetle is one of the smallest yet strongest animals in the world, capable of moving over 850 times its weight. Can you imagine that? If so, you may sense what Beetle knows: that we are all capable agents of change. So stop feeling small and making excuses, says Beetle. Utilize your unique skills to innovate or advocate.

BUTTERFLY

KEYS
- Beauty
- Patience
- Trust
- Transformation

TEACHING

Because they begin life as tiny wriggling caterpillars, butterflies are often associated with rebirth, change, and transformation. A profound mystery unfolds as the wormlike larvae seclude themselves into the sac of their chrysalis and, days to weeks later, unfurl their wings to become the beautiful creatures we call butterflies.

Butterfly teaches the wisdom of patience, reminding us to trust the process of change. By witnessing the drastic transition from larva to pupa to butterfly, we may be changed as well. Butterfly inspires us to unfold our imagination, open our wings, and embrace the greater possibilities of who we may become.

Butterflies smell with their antennae, drink nectar through their long proboscis, feel vibrations through their wings, and can see ultraviolet light.

Butterfly encourages us to perceive in new and different ways, to heighten the sensitivity of our senses, and to be attentive to nature's subtle yet powerful signs. Butterfly reminds us to uplift our thoughts so that we may recognize the stunning beauty and magic in our world.

QUESTIONS

Are you afraid to change? Is the idea of releasing the old too scary or traumatic? Are you frightened of what the new will bring? Butterfly gently and respectfully asks you to relax and allow. Imagine your fears as a flock of butterflies, fluttering through a field of flowers. A dependable and compassionate guide, Butterfly can help you lighten up and trust the process of change.

DRAGONFLY

KEYS

- ○━ Acrobatic flyer
- ○━ Holds ancient wisdom
- ○━ Connects dimensions
- ○━ Knows the power of inspiration

TEACHING

As one of the first winged insects to evolve on our planet, dragonflies carry ancient knowledge. Their slender body and two sets of gauzy wings look fragile, but are actually quite strong. Darting through the air, they glimmer with iridescence, offering quick glimpses of other times, other worlds. Dragonfly helps us recall old wisdom, when magic was alive.

Master acrobats, dragonflies hover, swoop, and glide. Their agile movements and vibrantly flashing colors represent flexibility to perceive myriad points of view. Dragonfly can help us travel lightly in other worlds, and return safely with bits of knowledge that we can use. Dragonfly teaches through streamlined, elegant, intuitive gleams of knowing.

Dragonflies have compound eyes. As with many insects, their vision is an assemblage of smaller visual units combined. Dragonfly's large, dark, shiny eyes hint at vast knowledge held within.

Dragonflies begin life as water nymphs, later shedding their skin and spreading their wings to fly. Linking water with air, Dragonfly directs our attention to the in-between, the sacred space where transformation occurs.

QUESTIONS

Does life seem dreary and uninspired? Have you lost your sense of wonder? Spend time with Dragonfly to recall the whispers from spirit that once reverberated within your heart. Dragonfly has a flair for awakening the inner muse. Sparking curiosity, awe, and fascination, Dragonfly stimulates the creative impulse so that you may shine brightly once again.

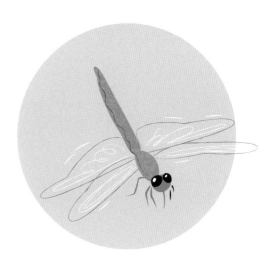

FIREFLY

Fireflies mostly use their light signals in mating ceremonies, which involve elaborate movements and correct timing. Male fireflies perform aerobatic maneuvers and females respond; both use flashes of light. Their illuminated pulses and patterns require precision, for only if the actions and responses are paired correctly will males and females come together.

Firefly reminds us to trust and honor our personal rhythms to find the one who is right for us. Firefly assures us that our desires will be answered when the time is right. Wise Firefly advises us not to settle for anything less.

KEYS

o—¬ Illuminates the night

o—¬ Invokes surprise and delight

o—¬ Understands the importance of timing

o—¬ Reminds us to sparkle

TEACHING

Members of the beetle family, fireflies light up the night with sparkles of wonder. Their lovely glow hints at insight and spiritual illumination. Sometimes known as lightning bugs, fireflies radiate small but intense luminescent colors—yellow, green, or pale red. Spirit of Firefly signals new ideas, inspiration, hope, and creative awakenings.

QUESTIONS

Do you wonder if you're on the right path? Are you looking for a sign? Firefly encourages you to keep the faith. We're all on the right path and our gifts are awakening. Meditate with Firefly to discover any hidden paths you may have overlooked. Shine your light to attract others of a similar vibration. Ordinary by day, sparkling with brilliance at night, Firefly will light your way with beauty. Follow Firefly to kindle your dreams and keep on glowing.

GRASSHOPPER

KEYS
- Lucky leaper
- Sensitive to surroundings
- Trusts instincts
- Advocates taking a chance

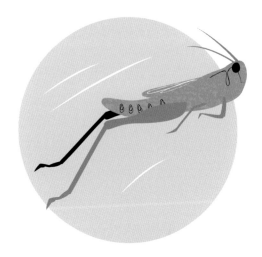

TEACHING

Associated with good luck, longevity, and happy news, Grasshopper encourages us to take a chance. Most known for their amazing leaps—up to 20 times their length—grasshoppers follow their instincts to jump quickly. Grasshopper helps us succeed in life by trusting our hunches and moving forward, never back.

There are over 11,000 types of grasshopper, and each species has its own song. Snapping their wings in flight or rubbing leg to wing to create a chirping noise, grasshoppers communicate with sound, gesture, and movement. Grasshopper invokes creative communication.

Grasshoppers use their impressive antennae—some as long as their body—to smell and sense the world. Grasshopper heightens awareness and advises us to be aware of our surroundings in more sensitive ways.

Though their long, strong legs allow splendid leaps into the air, grasshoppers land safely upon the earth. Grasshopper reminds us to ground our actions and anchor our lives with stability and security. Grasshopper reassures us that we are capable of amazing feats if we trust ourselves to leap.

QUESTIONS

Looking for luck or adventure? Grasshopper says, why not make your own? Grasshopper encourages forward thinking and bold decisions. Are you ready to aim high? Creative muse and intrepid instigator, Grasshopper can help you know when the time is right to make your giant leap forward. Be patient and alert. With Grasshopper beside you, your outcome is favorable.

LADYBUG

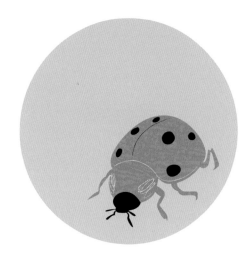

KEYS

○⊸ Good luck
○⊸ Prosperity
○⊸ Smooth transitions
○⊸ Love of life

TEACHING

A traditional sign of good luck and happiness, ladybugs are small beetles with domed backs, usually brightly colored red or yellow with black spots. Like all beetles, ladybugs undergo metamorphosis, transitioning from larva to pupa to winged insect. Ladybug reminds us that even small transformations can be profound.

There are over 5,000 species of ladybugs—also known as ladybird beetles. The name derives from the Middle Ages, when (the story goes) swarms of insects devastated crops. Prayers to the Virgin Mary were answered by ladybugs that ate the insects. Affectionately called beetles of Our Lady, they were viewed as good omens, associated with renewal, protection, and helpful change.

Though their bold coloring warns predators to stay away, it also reveals a playful spirit. The delightful form of ladybugs evokes smiles from children and adults alike. Ladybug's gentle manner nudges us to trust and enjoy our life. Ladybug knows that by staying true to who we are, good luck is ours.

QUESTIONS

Do you have insectophobia? Does the sight of creepy crawlies send you screaming? Ladybug offers its humble services. Alighting upon your hand, gently walking on your fingertip, Ladybug introduces you to the pleasurable joys of insects. No stingers, no frantic motions, no foreboding gaze— Ladybug says let go of preconceptions so that you may see with eyes of wonder. Ladybug awakens childlike curiosity and can help you perceive the beauty of all life.

MANTIS

KEYS

- ⊶ Master of movement
- ⊶ Accomplished warrior
- ⊶ Guide to higher dimensions of consciousness

TEACHING

The word mantis means prophet or seer—an appropriate name for this perceptive insect that can help us access higher dimensions of awareness. With its large eyes, long antennae, and oddly swiveling triangular face, Mantis seems from another world. That too is appropriate, for Mantis opens doorways of consciousness that lead to other realms.

There are over 2,300 species of mantis with wide variation in color, pattern, and name—dead leaf, unicorn, Egyptian pygmy and devil's flower are all types of mantis. Mantises are accomplished ambush hunters, waiting silently, sensing keenly before they strike. Springing into action in a flash, with a fine efficiency of movement, mantises take what they need. Elegant and poised—and highly skilled in the art of stealth—Mantis teaches attention, focus, and precision.

Sitting upright, folded forearms held aloft, mantises can be still and vigilant as ninjas. Calm, contemplative Mantis is an expert guide to deep meditation and inner-world journeys, pointing out portals that allow travel to distant realms.

QUESTIONS

Have you reached the limits in your area of expertise? Mantis is a special teacher, inviting only select students who are ready to refine their skills beyond the ordinary. You may first be tested for patience, agility of mind, and dedication. There are no guarantees. But if the doorway opens and Mantis beckons, you will be offered an extraordinary opportunity that bypasses knowledge and wisdom, and which may affect the very essence of your being.

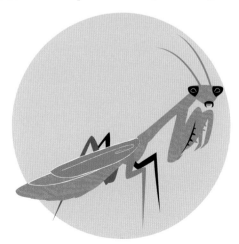

MOSQUITO

KEYS

○━ Persistent

○━ Practical

○━ Deepens our sense of connection

TEACHING

Skilled bloodsuckers that take without asking, mosquitos are not well loved by humans. Persistent in their speedy movements and vexing stings, a mosquito's annoying hum is the background noise we never want to hear. A little insect with a powerful teaching, Mosquito challenges us to look at why minor inconveniences in life can trigger such great frustration.

Of the more than 3,000 species of mosquito, only a few carry disease—but that's enough. The anopheles mosquito is solely responsible for malaria, one of the leading causes of death worldwide. Mosquito is living proof that the tiny is not to be taken lightly.

Using highly developed senses, mosquitos choose their targets carefully. Only females bite and suck blood—up to three times their body weight—which they use to nourish their eggs. Though mosquitos generally prefer the blood of horses, cattle, and birds, humans are acceptable—and so we become the unwitting donors that help to

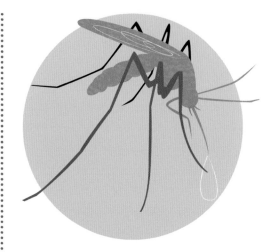

perpetuate the mosquito's cycle of life. Mosquito can help us realize that we are all more deeply interconnected than we may know.

QUESTIONS

Is something bugging you? Mosquito prods you to pay attention to that which annoys or gets under your skin. Minor annoyances are often a cover for something bigger and more deeply rooted in the psyche. Are you ready to accept the ramifications of what study with Mosquito may entail? Delivered with a sting and an itchy red reminder, Mosquito's teaching forces us to face reality.

MOTH

KEYS
- Teacher of transition
- Offers night wisdom
- Awakens our subtle senses

TEACHING

There are well over 100,000 species of moth, each with unique abilities. Some moths are large, spectacularly colored, and active during the day. Most moths, however, are small with muted colors, and nocturnal. In some cultures moths are believed to be messengers from the spirit realm or souls of the recently departed. Often associated with death, Moth assists in transitions between worlds.

Fluttering through the night sky to gather flower nectar, moths are guided by the light of the moon. Spirit of Moth heightens intuition and psychic abilities, helping us to sense in subtle ways, to be more keenly aware of shadow realms, and to better navigate in the dark.

Experts at camouflage, moths can blend into backgrounds, as if invisible. Moth knows the value of disguise and the power of stillness. But sometimes moths want to be noticed. Female moths release powerful pheromones, creating scent trails that males follow over long distances. Moth awakens our senses, refining our awareness in this world and others.

QUESTIONS

One of the few insects that have scales covering their wings, moths also have sensitive feathery antennae and can coil up their proboscis—feeding tube—when not in use. What special skills do you have? Moth encourages you to pay attention to dormant abilities that may prove helpful as you expand awareness and deepen in spiritual development. An excellent guide to contemplating secret knowledge, Moth advises you to acknowledge, appreciate, and utilize your inner gifts.

SCORPION

KEYS

o—• Protective

o—• Supports change

o—• Uncovers secrets

TEACHING

With their hardened exoskeleton, strong pincers, and venomous stinger, scorpions embody the art of protection. Cunning and calculating, they know how to defend and when to attack. Vigilant in their surroundings and alert to prey, scorpions use stealth and strength to accomplish their goals.

Because they have poor eyesight, scorpions generally wait for their prey. Expertly poised with raised stinger and menacing pincers, Scorpion teaches both how to keep others away and when to strike. In mythology, scorpions guard sacred gateways. In some cultures, they are fashioned into amulets, worn to ward off evil.

Members of the arachnid family, scorpions shed their exoskeletons several times before reaching adulthood. A potent symbol of death and rebirth, Scorpion knows the importance of shedding the old so that new growth may occur. Scorpion opens us to change.

There is something secretive about Scorpion. Sensing with fine hairs and special organs on their legs, scorpions are sensitive to touch and vibrations. Scorpion sharpens our instincts to find what is hidden, and hones our intuition to uncover what we need to know.

QUESTIONS

Feeling vulnerable and unprotected? Or, are you overprotective and excessively defensive? Scorpion aids not only to repel negative energies and keep harmful influences away, but also to release paranoid feelings of fear or persecution. Like many insects, Scorpion's teaching touches on transformation. Call upon Scorpion to help you rearrange your outlook and create inner balance so that you may see clearly and move forward safely.

SPIDER

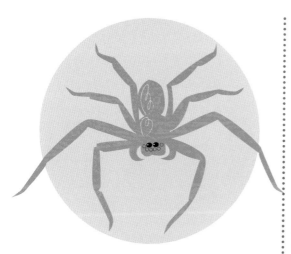

KEYS

O—⊸ Master weaver

O—⊸ Awakens creativity

O—⊸ Spins infinite possibilities

TEACHING

A trickster, a creator, a weaver of fates, Spider is seen in different ways to different cultures. Credited with designing the grand plan of existence, Spider spins a web of beauty and intrigue. Known as the keeper of words and originator of the primordial alphabet, Spider facilitates translation, interpretation, and pattern recognition.

Found in nearly every habitat, and with 35,000 species worldwide, spiders are incredibly versatile. They range widely in color, size, and web design. With bodies shaped like figure eights, spiders have eight legs and usually eight eyes as well. The number links Spider to balance, geometry, and the mystery of infinity. Spider reminds us of the elegant ways in which all life is interconnected.

Most spiders create silk to weave webs, upon which they capture prey. Delicate and beautiful, spider silk is also extremely strong. Essential to spider survival, webs inspire us with their exquisite beauty. The cosmic master weaver, Spider reminds us to stay centered and attuned as we fabricate our lives.

QUESTIONS

Unhappy with your life? Or, are you content with the way your plans are unfolding? Either way, Spider reminds you that you are the creator of your reality. Our webs can entangle—others as well as ourselves—or help us attain what we need. Spider advises you to take responsibility for your actions, for all you do is a thread of creation that affects what happens next. Spider knows that our choices determine our future.

REPTILES & WATER ANIMALS

KEYS

- Navigate emotional realm
- Assist in transformation
- Expand awareness
- Deepen wisdom
- Celebrate joy

ALLIGATOR

KEYS

○—➤ Heightens perception
○—➤ Detects deceit
○—➤ Encourages emotional depth
○—➤ Awakens ancient wisdom

TEACHING

As the world's largest reptile and last living link to the prehistoric age of dinosaurs, Alligator offers a powerful connection to our own primal self. Alligators are extremely perceptive, with keen hearing and the ability to see above and below the waterline. This hints at one of their core teachings: to recognize the clarity of truth in both conscious and unconscious realms.

Just as its physical form is strong, armored, and formidable, Alligator's guidance is no-nonsense and not for the faint of heart. Indeed, Alligator's teaching can be sharp as it exposes pretense and self-deception. Are you willing to see your true self? If so, Alligator can be a superb guide in helping you to discover who you really are.

Attentive to the cycles of birth and death, creation and destruction, Alligator possesses a strong-minded medicine of permanent change and transformation. Guardian of ancient truths, Alligator encourages us to rely upon our own knowledge by accessing innate wisdom that resides within.

QUESTIONS

If Alligator arrives, you may be asked to take a deep, honest look in the mirror. What am I hiding from myself? What prevents me from being who I really am? Alligator encourages us to release what is fraudulent and no longer useful in order to pursue our soul's desire. Are you ready to move through your fears so that greater awareness may emerge? Alligator watches and waits.

CRAB

KEYS

○━┓ Understands protection

○━┓ Steps sideways

○━┓ Supports cycles of change

○━┓ Coaxes us out of our shells

TEACHING

Generally shy and sensitive, crabs hide within their shells—hard exoskeletons which serve to shield their tender bodies and provide shelter and safety as well. Living in all the world's oceans as well as in freshwater and on land, crabs are a widespread symbol of protection.

As crabs begin to outgrow their shells, they molt. Soaking up seawater, crabs swell until they burst through their shells. Initially soft and vulnerable, they must wait until their new shell hardens. Symbolic of rebirth and necessary change, Crab assists with transitions and prods us to come out of our shell in order to grow. Crab teaches us to trust cycles of change and accept the inevitability of transformation.

Crabs communicate by tapping and waving their pincers. Most crabs move neither forward nor back, but in a sideways fashion. Crab reminds us that sometimes the best route is not one we expect. Crab can help us to be flexible and express ourselves in unusual ways. Crab encourages us to find our own unique ways to success.

QUESTIONS

Are you withdrawn and reclusive? Crab understands how vulnerable you can feel, exposing yourself to the world. But Crab also knows that life requires change. Trust Crab to come out of your shell and try on some new ways of being that also offer safety and protection. Sidestep with Crab to relax into the natural flow of transformation.

DOLPHIN

KEYS

- Playful swimmers
- Interdimensional travelers
- Mirrors to humanity

TEACHING

Intelligent and friendly, dolphins travel the world's oceans, carrying deep knowledge of the sea. Some say dolphins are from other worlds, emissaries of higher consciousness, visiting Earth to help us evolve. Once believed to be messengers from water gods, known to help sailors and travelers, dolphins help us find our way home.

Living in large social groups, dolphins form strong alliances and lasting friendships. Traveling, fishing, or nurturing their young, dolphins delight in leaping together and having fun. Expressive and curious, Dolphin encourages us to play and celebrate the thrills of life.

It is easy to love dolphins for their exuberant leaps and joyful spirit. But dolphins also express anger and can be bullies and violent toward others. Spirit of Dolphin mirrors our humanity, reminding us of the best and worst of who we are. Dolphin encourages us to explore our dark depths and bring emotional wounds to the surface for healing. Dolphin inspires us to better express the fullness of who we are.

QUESTIONS

Dolphins communicate in many ways— they whistle and click, blow bubbles and slap their tails, use echolocation and sound waves too. Are you finding creative ways to express yourself to the world? Dolphin reminds you that sounds and body movements can be tools to heal and influence others in positive ways. Dolphin nudges you to reveal your truth, voice your love, and live in joy.

FROG

At home both on land and in water, Frog awakens our creative nature, brings artistic ideas to the surface, and helps ground our dreams in reality. Representing the fluid nature of metamorphosis, Frog can help us move smoothly from one stage of life to another.

With excellent depth perception, sensitive hearing, and fast, sticky tongues, frogs are skilled at catching prey. Frog aids in elevating perceptions and accelerating movement. Frog is also associated with healing, medicine, and altered states of consciousness. Frog enhances intuition, shares secrets of the spirit realm, and helps travelers return safely home.

KEYS

○—ᴇ Jumps into change

○—ᴇ Helps ease transition

○—ᴇ Brings healing

○—ᴇ Advocates adaptability

TEACHING

Associated with happiness, good luck, abundance, and fertility, frogs jump into our lives as symbolic agents of change. Adaptable and diverse, frogs have lived on Earth for 350 million years. Linked to magic and transformation, Frog can help us leap successfully through transitions of status, age, or consciousness.

Frogs are amphibians. Beginning life as eggs in water, they hatch into tiny tadpoles, and later develop into frogs.

QUESTIONS

In the midst of a major life transition? Struggling to slide into your new identity? Frog is a master at easing the shifts of change. A good power animal for those who are uncertain or anxious around change, Frog can help you stay flexible and adaptable, and trust the process of transformation. Take a leap with Frog to embrace the new.

GOLDFISH

KEYS
- Joy
- Peace
- Beauty
- Tranquillity

TEACHING

First domesticated in China over 1,000 years ago, goldfish symbolize good luck and fortune. Though wild goldfish tend to be darkly colored, centuries of breeding have transformed domesticated goldfish into the brightly colored and unusually shaped aquarium and ornamental pond residents we know today. Believed to bring prosperity, peace, and balanced energy to one's home, goldfish swim into our lives with joy.

Incredibly adaptive, goldfish are clever and have good vision. Some interact with humans through hand-feeding and can perform tricks. Dazzling orange, yellow, red, and white, with fancy tails, bubble eyes, and metallic sheen, goldfish calm and fascinate us with their shimmery movements.

Meditate with Goldfish to enter fluid inner realms of self, access deep emotions, and swim through the psyche.

Goldfish advises us to relax deeply and marvel at the beauty of diverse colors, shapes, and forms that may initiate altered states of perception. Goldfish animates our imagination and helps us to expand our appreciation of life.

QUESTIONS

So seemingly ordinary, available at any pet store, Goldfish has a secret teaching. Did you suspect? Goldfish invites you to embrace your daydreams so that you may replenish creativity and experience deep peace of being. More than that, Goldfish can help you float inner-world experiences up to the surface of consciousness so that you may share them with others. Be like Goldfish—splash your tail and shimmer your love to inspire others and enjoy yourself.

HIPPOPOTAMUS

KEYS

○—⚹ Defends home

○—⚹ Protects family

○—⚹ Helps access emotional realm

TEACHING

Large lovers of water, hippos spend most of their days submerged in rivers and ponds. Their name means water horse, and they are the second biggest mammal on land. Despite their stocky shape, hippos are surprisingly agile; they can turn quickly and easily outrun a human.

While they may look placid sunning in shallow waters, hippos are territorial and one of the most dangerous animals in Africa. Known for aggressively protecting themselves and their families, hippos teach respect and defense.

Congregating peacefully in water—which amplifies their feelings of togetherness—hippos enjoy each other's company. At dusk, however, they forge and follow their own trails to graze in solitude throughout the night. Hippo reminds us to appreciate time with others and cherish our time alone.

With a bit of buoyancy, hippos move nimbly along the water bottom. Whether accessing deep feelings in our emotional realm or awakening intimate connections with others, Hippo can help us to travel lightly yet feel stable and secure.

QUESTIONS

Always daydreaming? Do you lose yourself in creative imaginings? Perhaps Hippo can help. With nostrils and eyes positioned high upon their heads, hippos submerge in water yet remain fully aware of what's happening above. Follow Hippo's lead to enjoy your inner wanderings without losing perspective of reality. Well-rounded and happy, Hippo can help you access creative realms while still maintaining your outlook on life.

JELLYFISH

KEYS

- Transparent
- Inspires wandering
- Helps us to accept what is

TEACHING

Jellyfish, also known as jellies, are not fish, but marine animals with a gelatinous bell and trailing tentacles. With bells as small as thimbles or larger than humans, jellyfish use their tentacles—which can reach a stunning 120 feet in length — to sting and capture prey. A very old species, jellyfish are found in every ocean, floating upon the surface or pulsing deep within the dark.

Largely transparent, with no blood, brain, or nervous system, jellyfish are 95 percent water. Limited in mobility, jellies are largely captives of winds, tides, and currents. Sensitive to water energies and feelings, Jellyfish teaches us to go with the flow and accept circumstances over which we have no control.

Often traveling in large groups called blooms, jellies produce bioluminescent light in a variety of intense colors— bright red, vibrant purple, hot pink, and pearly white. While their otherworldly shapes fascinate and inspire, Jellyfish reminds us to shine our own inner light and wisdom. Jellyfish prompts us to be illumined.

QUESTIONS

Angry? Obsessive? Knotted up with anxiety? Breathe deeply and float with Jellyfish to calm your mind. As you drift, feel your body ease and soften. Jellyfish encourages you to let go of thoughts that harden and depress. Be gentle with yourself and enjoy the natural flow of energy. Jellyfish knows that as you relax and allow, you will feel more at home and accepting of the changing currents of life.

LIZARD

KEYS

- ○—⚡ Master dreamer
- ○—⚡ Teaches adaptability
- ○—⚡ Deepens perceptions
- ○—⚡ Helps us to let go

TEACHING

Cold-blooded with scales and tails, there are over 5,000 species of lizard. Some change color, some have horns, and some are over nine feet long. Most have four legs, though some have two, and some have none at all. Diverse and adaptable, lizards can glide through the air, skitter over water, and shed their tails if caught by a predator.

Lizard teaches us how to adapt to a variety of situations and act accordingly.

With excellent vision and hearing, lizards are sensitive to vibrations as well. Spirit of Lizard heightens perceptions, stimulates psychic abilities, and can help us see into the future. Journey with Lizard to discover alternate ways of perceiving reality.

Traditionally associated with dreamtime, Lizard assists in recalling dreams as well as initiating and maintaining lucid dream states. An astute teacher skilled in navigating through unusual realms of awareness, Lizard helps to clarify perceptions and bring insights to waking life. Lizard urges us both to respect and utilize the wisdom offered by dreams and other inner-world journeys.

QUESTIONS

Has Lizard shown up in your life? If so, it may be time to make a change. Lizard prods you to take a good look at the different paths or possibilities before you. Lizard can help you travel down each to perceive its outcome before choosing what to do. What a trick! Lizard prompts you to evaluate options carefully and consider wisely before making your move.

MANATEE

KEYS

- Peaceful
- Loving
- Advocates kindness
- Emanates peace

TEACHING

Once mistaken for mermaids, manatees are also known as sea cows—though their closest living relatives are elephants. Shaped like submarines, weighing over half a ton, manatees are extremely gentle, slow-moving, vegetarian sea mammals.

Despite their immensity, manatees are graceful swimmers, using their strong tails to leisurely propel them forward. Floating in calm, shallow, warm-water bays, lagoons, rivers, and canals, manatees spend their days eating, resting, exploring, and bonding with their pod. An easygoing and pleasurable traveling companion, Manatee reminds us to slow down, take our time, have fun, and enjoy life.

Curious and inquisitive, manatees enjoy playing games and using their sensitive mouths to investigate and eat grasses. Friendly, loving, protective, and nurturing to their young, manatees also allow humans to swim near. Manatee teaches compassion and trust.

An ancient species, manatees have good long-term memories and knowledge of early oceanic life. Helping us to recall deep wisdom, Manatee nudges us to embrace the Earth and all her inhabitants with kindness and with love.

QUESTIONS

Feeling heavy? It may seem funny that such a large and weighty animal can help you to feel lighter, but such is the buoyant spirit of Manatee. Close your eyes and glide with Manatee. Do you feel supported by the warm healing waters, comforted and protected by your proximity to this gentle giant? Inspiring affection and lightness of being, bighearted Manatee assures you that you are loved.

OCTOPUS

KEYS

- ⚬—⚊ Intelligent
- ⚬—⚊ Strategic
- ⚬—⚊ Creative
- ⚬—⚊ Master of camouflage

TEACHING

With no skeleton, eight tentacles, three hearts, and blue-colored blood, Octopus does not fail to amaze. Nocturnal and most often solitary, octopuses live on the bottom of the ocean floor and are thus familiar with the mysteries of the deep. Both curious and creative, they love to explore their environment, solve problems, and investigate how things work.

Highly astute, octopuses learn by observation as well as experience. They use shells as tools and sometimes arrange found objects as "gardens" around their lairs. Adaptable and highly intelligent, Octopus advises us to be flexible when responding to new situations, to pay attention to others for helpful tips, to use our intellect to strategize, and to remain open to life's possibilities.

With specialized muscles that affect cell pigment, octopuses can quickly change their skin color, pattern, and texture to camouflage and hide in plain sight.

Fast and clever, they elude enemies by releasing clouds of dark ink that dull their predator's sense of sight and smell. A talented escape artist and master of disguise, Octopus confuses those who would cause it harm and teaches us the secret of a good getaway.

QUESTIONS

Feeling daring? Octopus challenges you to explore the motion of emotion. Study with Octopus to develop fluidity with your feelings so that you may adapt swiftly to shifting currents of change and better sail through stormy seas. Octopus can help you navigate the depths of your emotional realm with agility and ease.

OTTER

With webbed feet, powerful tails, and a passion for swimming, otters love water, though most species make their homes on land. Found in rivers, lakes, ponds, and oceans, they enliven their habitats with free-spirited antics. Otter reminds us to let go, accept our circumstances and enjoy our lives. Otter renews our spirit with joy.

Friendly and helpful to others, otters enjoy group merriment. Otter advocates good hospitality and good-natured games. A helpful power animal to protect and inspire one's inner child, Otter recommends a well-rounded life that celebrates laughter and fun.

KEYS

○━ Lighthearted
○━ Curious
○━ Playful
○━ Fun

TEACHING

Energetic acrobats with boundless enthusiasm, otters chase and slide, splash and glide, turn somersaults, float on their backs, and dive for food. Long, agile, sleek, and limber, otters cannot help moving with grace and ease. Naturally inquisitive and lively with creative thoughts, they explore their environment and find ways to have fun. Otter awakens curiosity, stimulates our sense of wonder, and reminds us that life is full of playful opportunities.

QUESTIONS

Mistrustful of others? Prone to jealousy? Traditionally associated with the feminine, Otter can help you balance envy, suspicion, and resentment with a softer outlook on life. Otter encourages you to see others as you would like to be seen. What about sharing, giving, nurturing, and loving from the heart? Swim with Otter to lighten up heavy feelings and brighten your perspective in order to more fully enjoy yourself and those around you.

SALMON

KEYS

○━ Perseverance

○━ Overcomes obstacles

○━ Helps us return home

TEACHING

Fish are traditionally symbols of wisdom, fertility, longevity, and prosperity. Salmon is a particularly powerful fish, often believed to awaken wisdom through visits from the spirit realm.

Born in freshwater, salmon migrate to the ocean, where they spend most of their lives before returning to their birthplace to reproduce. Some salmon travel almost 1,000 miles in order to spawn. It's a difficult journey swimming upstream, encountering rocks, waterfalls, predators, and ever-changing currents. Leaping over obstacles, Spirit of Salmon encourages us to persist and overcome difficulties with steadfast determination.

On returning to their spawning ground, salmon lay their eggs and die. It's a powerful cycle that begins and ends in the same place. Linking the fertilization of new ideas with the conclusion of old, Salmon helps us to be courageous as we move through cycles of change that demand our presence. Inspiring visions of success and the promise of completion, Salmon helps us to trust our inner knowing on the journey home to self.

QUESTIONS

Nearing the end of a life transition or spiritual journey? Salmon knows that coming home to self brings great insight, wisdom, and deep knowledge. It may require time, however, to fully comprehend and apply what you've learned. Salmon brings clarity and meaning so that you may better understand your experiences and share them with others. Dream with Salmon to learn how to integrate deep-self wisdom into everyday life.

SEAHORSE

KEYS
- Protection
- Patience
- Anchor
- Vision

TEACHING

With its curled tail, bony plates of armor, and horselike head, Seahorse is whimsical and distinct. Once regarded as tiny sea dragons, seahorses were also believed to lead the souls of drowned sailors to the underworld. A symbol of power, luck, and guidance, Seahorse offers transport to distant realms and safe passage through emotional seas.

Found in calm, shallow, tropical waters, seahorses find coral reefs and sheltered areas to rest. Slowly propelled by their fins, seahorses swim upright. Roamers of the sea, they are patient and easygoing. Spirit of Seahorse teaches us to slow down and be happy where we are. If waters become turbulent, seahorses wrap their tail around nearby objects. Seahorse demonstrates how to anchor ourselves through life's stormy seas, advising us to hold on until the current passes.

Seahorses have excellent eyesight and can move each eye independently. Capable of seeing in opposite directions simultaneously, Seahorse reminds us to look around when we are lost or uncertain. Seahorse can help us expand our views by perceiving all sides of a situation.

QUESTIONS

Did you know that female seahorses impregnate the males? It's true; females deposit up to 1,500 eggs in a male's pouch, where they remain until birth. Is it time you shake up traditional notions of male and female responsibilities or consider sharing duties with your partner in a different way? Seahorse invites you to consider alternate perspectives in relationships and in life.

SEAL

Graceful in water, seals are lively and like to have fun. When playful, Seal inspires us to feel comfortable in our body and at home in our emotions. Seals can dive very deep—down to 4,000 feet—and stay submerged for hours. When serious, Seal pulls us down into neglected memories of our subconscious.

An expert guide to lucid dreaming, Seal can also help us remember dreams that feel too heavy to bring to consciousness. Seal has skills traveling through inner oceans of awareness, and can teach us to integrate distant realms of consciousness. Seal nudges us to uncover the deeper mysteries of self.

KEYS

○┬ Knows secrets
○┬ Helps us go deep
○┬ Skilled in lucid dreaming
○┬ Uncovers mysteries

TEACHING

With their large eyes and habit of bobbing their head above water to observe, seals are believed to perceive secret knowledge. In legend, seals are linked to the shape-shifting selkies, who live both as humans and as seals. Traditionally known as keepers of wisdom, Seal can help us discover what is forgotten or hidden in the depths of our being.

QUESTIONS

What's your innermost desire? Seal understands deep longing and the importance of our soul's yearning. Dive deep with Seal to access your forgotten dreams and bring them back to land. Seal can help you remember what was once important and vital to your being. Seal can also help you break through judgments—from others or yourself—that caused you to forget. Seal brings healing through fulfillment.

SHARK

KEYS

- Intelligent survivor
- Moves forward
- Sees clearly
- Trusts self

TEACHING

Sleek and streamlined, sharks have been evolving for over 400 million years. There are currently about 500 species of shark, including the immense 20-ton whale shark—at 40 feet, the longest fish in the world. Holding ancient wisdom, Shark is intelligent, keenly observant, and a master of survival.

Curious, calculating, and highly efficient, sharks patrol the world's oceans taking what they need.

Though they top the underwater food chain, sharks often eat the sick and dead. Shark helps us to see opportunity and adapt. Because they will sink when motionless, sharks are constantly moving. Shark reminds us to keep going and maintain forward momentum.

Possessing excellent sensory abilities, sharks can detect subtle vibrations and energy meridians upon the ocean floor. Spirit of Shark recommends sharpening perceptions and fine-tuning discernment. With cool control, Shark can help us navigate inner realms with accuracy and heightened awareness. Master of emotional stability, Shark teaches us to glide successfully through the turbulence of life by keeping our minds clear and our feelings centered.

QUESTIONS

Ever see a shark smile? All those teeth! Does it make you frightened or are you curious about what exists beneath appearances? Shark can help you see clearly and accurately. With skilled precision, Shark directs you to pierce irrational fears and confront the ones that hold you back. Swim with Shark to deepen self-reliance, expand personal power, and better know yourself—with a smile.

SNAIL

KEYS

- Patient
- Protective
- Tactile
- Timeless

TEACHING

Small and ubiquitous, snails have been gliding upon Earth's surface for about 500 million years. Found nearly everywhere—on land, in plants, in freshwater, and deep within the salty sea—water snails and land snails make their presence known.

Using a pore near their mouth to emit mucous, snails slide easily upon their silvery trails. Incredibly tactile, they press and contract their long, tender bodies upon the surface of wherever they roam. Snail helps us reconnect with the Earth, to immerse ourselves in the textures of kinesthetic feeling. Snail helps us appreciate the sensuous aspects of life and find pleasure in touch.

Snail's shell features a spiral design, symbolic of life spiraling outwards, evolution unfurling. Associated with the moon, fertility, and cycles of change, Snail helps us to contemplate the spiritual growth of our soul.

Moving calmly and leisurely, snails are very, very patient. A gentle guide that never hurries, Snail invites us to slow down and feel the earth. Snail nudges us to open our senses so that we may know ourselves and our planet in deeper, more intimate ways.

QUESTIONS

Would you like to feel at home—safe yet comfortable—wherever you travel? Slide beside Snail to instill a deep sense of centeredness within your body and mind. Snail can teach you how to feel secure while still being open and in close touch with your surroundings, no matter where you roam.

SNAKE

KEYS

○—→ Guards sacred spaces
○—→ Awakens latent energy
○—→ Initiates spiritual transformation

TEACHING

In ancient cultures, snakes were revered as powerful symbols of creation, wisdom, transformation, and immortality. Linked to gods and goddesses, kings and queens, Snake protected and advised. Some humans connect Snake with temptation and death. Both feared and worshipped, Snake is a no-nonsense teacher that demands our attention and respect.

Snakes have no eyelids, so their eyes are always open. That is why some believe snakes to be seers. Linked to prophecy, all-seeing Snake sharpens our perceptions and helps us to perceive in other worlds. Snakes also shed their skin several times a year—a reminder to shed old ways of being so that we may grow in bigger, brighter ways.

Coiling and wrapping, sliding and slithering, snakes are linked to sexuality and primal energies. Snake embodies kundalini, the latent energy force coiled at the base of our spine. Initiating expansions of consciousness and helping us to better feel and understand energy flows within the body, Snake is a healer, guardian, and skilled mentor offering lessons on the mysteries of life, death, and spiritual awakening.

QUESTIONS

Snake guards your most sacred treasure—that which you most fear and that which you most desire. If the time is right, Snake may lead you there. Striking with power and precision, Snake's initiation is a quick hit that sharpens awareness and triggers enlightenment, unlocking the mystery of who you really are. Are you ready for such a profound transformation?

STARFISH

Diverse in color, size, and shape, most starfish have five arms, though some have up to 40. Linking oceanic realms of consciousness with spiritual wisdom, Starfish stimulates our imagination and initiates mystical knowledge. Wriggling arms sprawling outward in celestial splendor, Starfish helps us to sense and dream in bigger ways.

Although they have no brains or blood, starfish have nerves that stretch to the tips of their limbs, ending in tiny eyes. Starfish helps to awaken sensory sensitivity—including extrasensory perception—so that we may see, feel, and know the world in deeper ways. Famous for their ability to regenerate a lost limb, starfish are also symbols of renewal and rejuvenation. Starfish reminds us that even if all seems lost, we can regain what we need to survive.

KEYS

- Symbol of renewal
- Aids regeneration
- Encourages us to feel

TEACHING

Beautiful and mysterious, starfish—sometimes called sea stars—inspire wonder and delight. Over 2,000 species of starfish have been found across all the oceans, in warm water and cold, in tidal areas as well as deep on the seafloor. Once considered light-bearing guides that helped lost sailors find their way home, starfish represent safe travel upon the sea.

QUESTIONS

With thousands of tiny tubes on the underside of their arms, starfish feel everything they encounter. Spirit of Starfish wonders, might you open your senses in more perceptive ways? Starfish encourages you to fine-tune your feelings and engage subtle levels of awareness so that you may move forward with greater sensitivity and joy.

TURTLE

KEYS

- Guardian of Earth wisdom
- Longevity
- Protection
- Persistence

TEACHING

The name "turtle" is used in different ways in different regions. In general, there are three types of turtles: those that live near or in freshwater (terrapins and turtles), those that live in seawater (sea turtles), and those that live only on land (tortoises). Each turtle has its own talents, though all share in Turtle's teaching.

Some humans once imagined the Earth rested upon the back of a great turtle. Believed to be wise because of their longevity and calm acceptance of life, turtles are associated with healing and planetary knowledge. In close contact with the land, turtles offer grounded insights and common sense. Turtle also reminds us to honor and take care of our home.

Residing on this planet for millions of years, turtles persist with their slow and steady pace. Safe within their shells, they represent security and protection, and enjoy the benefit of being at home wherever they go. Turtle teaches us to take things slowly, follow our own rhythm, and draw upon Earth's healing energy to prosper. This is how we grow old and wise, like Turtle.

QUESTIONS

Turtles know exactly when to withdraw into their shells. How about you? Turtle reminds you to shield yourself from negativity, threat, and harm. In addition, Turtle recommends going within to contemplate, dream, rest, and heal. Take a tip from Turtle and remember not only to withdraw in times of danger, but also to replenish and renew.

SEA TURTLE

KEYS
- ○—ᴛ Skilled navigator
- ○—ᴛ Anchors ancient wisdom
- ○—ᴛ Deepens consciousness

TEACHING

Just as Turtle protects the Earth, Sea Turtle guards the sea. Well adapted for aquatic life, sea turtles evolved their long feet into flippers and streamlined their shell and body to propel gracefully through the water. Finely tuned to water energies, creativity, and the fluidity of feelings, Sea Turtle teaches us to swim smoothly in emotional waters and navigate confidently through oceanic realms of awareness.

Though they enjoy basking at the water's surface, sea turtles rarely leave their ocean home except to lay eggs. Mother turtles bury their eggs in sand and depend upon sunshine to warm and hatch their babies. Sea Turtle reminds us to protect, ground, and nurture new ideas before bringing them into the light.

Some believe sea turtles anchor dormant energies that will activate planetary awakening when the time is right. Journey with Sea Turtle to discover sacred portals that open to oceanic wisdom. Sea Turtle encourages us to sink down, embrace our deep self, and experience the fullness of who we are.

QUESTIONS

Are you navigating through stormy seas? Not sure which way to go? Close your eyes and ask Sea Turtle for some pointers on when to float and when to dive. Sea Turtle may advise you to sink into contemplation, move forward with focus, or open yourself to the healing energy of the seas. Spend time with Sea Turtle to observe, listen, and learn so that you may better know your path and purpose.

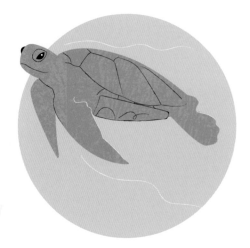

WHALE

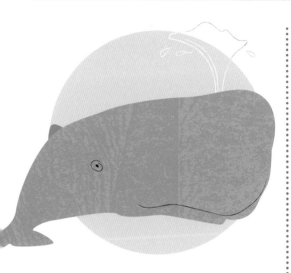

KEYS

o—⊶ Deep wisdom
o—⊶ Expansive energy
o—⊶ Attunes us to love

TEACHING

As the largest mammal on Earth, Whale's teaching is vast. Traveling the world's oceans, Whale's many species are unique and majestic—from spiral-tusked narwhals and Arctic white belugas to the immense blue whales, over 100 feet long. Holding expansive knowledge and ancient memories, Whale is the record keeper of Earth's wisdom.

Possessing strong fins and powerful tails, whales can both dive deep and leap upward to the sky. Sometimes seen as representatives of distant stars or intermediaries between Earth and other planets, Whale links realms. Inspiring us with their size, power, grace, and beauty, whales help us to dream big. Journey with Whale to explore inner worlds, open up to larger energies, and connect with other dimensional realities.

Extremely intelligent with a range of emotions, whales travel far and wide. Their good hearing and powerful lungs allow them to communicate with underwater sounds that can be heard for miles. Using special sound frequencies to heal and enlighten, Spirit of Whale attunes us to deeper vibrations, helping us love ourselves and resonate with the heartbeat of the Universe.

QUESTIONS

Are you up for a very special adventure? Long known as an emissary to distant galaxies, Whale offers a journey to realms unknown that may far exceed your capacity to imagine. Just as Whale can help you deepen in awareness, this wise cetacean can help you open to cosmic consciousness as well. If you're ready, Whale offers one wild ride that is out of this world.

CHAPTER FIVE

THE KEY TO
INTEGRATION

- ⚷— Deepen relationships and develop partnerships with animal spirits

....

- ⚷— Share consciousness to experience reality from an animal's perspective

....

- ⚷— Integrate animal teachings into everyday life

....

- ⚷— Encourage and inspire others by sharing your experiences

....

- ⚷— Give back to life in heartfelt ways

DEEPENING RELATIONSHIP

You've met some of your animal guides and have learned to interpret their messages. You've explored the teachings of spirit animals and have experimented with creative ways of bringing their energy into everyday life. You've opened your awareness and deepened your presence. Are you ready to work with animals in more conscious ways as partners, collaborators, and respected friends?

FLYING WITH RAVEN

I am a fan of Raven. I especially love watching these dark, majestic corvids swoop and dive upon thermals when the weather is windy. Associated with secrets and magic, ravens were once believed to serve as messengers between humans and the spirit world. Also known as shape-shifters, they sometimes invite us to better understand their views by merging consciousness and experiencing life through their perspective.

Fly with Raven to expand awareness and explore new realms.

Several times I have seen through Raven's eyes and felt through its body. I recall the pressure of air against my face, feeling the movement of Raven's strong, streamlined body, raising or lowering our wings to sail effortlessly and become one with the wind. I have sailed with ravens, circling thermals, dipping a wing to find the sweet spot in which we hover motionless.

Sliding into Raven's consciousness is an exercise in letting go, suspending human notions of gravity, and opening to the freedom of flight. It requires releasing rational thought for a time. You must trust and let go in order to feel the way the air cups your belly, how it pushes up like a soft cushion, supporting you, through the full width of outstretched wings.

The deeper and more intimately we open to animals, the more we align with their spiritual essence. By experiencing the way an animal moves and thinks and feels we come to know that animal within ourselves, thus expanding who we are and who we can become.

MERGING AWARENESS

There are many ways to connect with animals: observing, conversing, playing, honoring. One of my favorite ways to connect is by sharing consciousness—actually merging with an animal's thoughts, feelings, and sensory perceptions. It's as if you become a copilot of consciousness, aware of all that is happening from that animal's perspective. Not only does this type of sharing allow us to deepen in understanding of an animal's world, but it may open us to a new type of partnership.

I once learned to sniff with ursine sensitivity and hear the voice of the Arctic sea ice by sharing consciousness with a polar bear. It was an amazing experience, to be sure, but I also learned an equally amazing truth. To understand the world from an animal's perspective is not only to see another point of view, but also to change the way we experience reality.

It may feel as if you are imagining things in the beginning. In my experience, however, something remarkable occurs when we merge consciousness with another being. As with Raven, I didn't simply see from a higher perspective (though there was that too), I saw with a different type of clarity—a quality of vision that was altogether different from human perception.

I encourage you to try the following meditation with a variety of animals so that you may fully appreciate the wide range of unique perspectives in our world. Consider the possibilities: to run with Panther, fly with Flamingo, spin a web with Spider, and leap from the water with Whale.

To begin, however, you may want to choose a familiar spirit animal, one that you have worked with before and have come to trust.

Polar Bear is a skilled dreamer, creative teacher, and well-respected guide.

SHARING CONSCIOUSNESS MEDITATION

1. Close your eyes and relax. Breathe easily, in and out. As in previous meditations, allow your breath to connect you with the Earth, grounding your body in a safe, comfortable way. Also use your breath to connect with the Sky, feeling the freedom of expansion. [3 minutes.]

2. Invite your spirit animal to be present in your mind's eye. Slowly and respectfully, begin to connect, mind to mind, heart to heart, allowing the familiar energy of deep connection to link you with your animal partner. [2 minutes.]

3. When you are ready, ask your animal if you may share consciousness. Make sure you feel centered, that your animal agrees to this adventure, and that the circumstances feel right . . .

4. If all is well, deepen your breathing and allow your consciousness to expand even further. Open yourself slowly, steadily, until your awareness merges with your animal friend. [2 minutes.]

5. It may feel as if you are slipping inside your spirit animal's body, as if you are in the passenger seat of their sensory awareness. You are a visitor, a welcomed guest, and you may sense a greeting of welcome from your animal, an acknowledgment that you are present . . .

6. Continuing to breathe easily, in close connection with your animal, you may find you are now able to see and feel the world from your animal's point of view. Perhaps you can taste and hear from your animal's perspective . . .

7. Take some time to observe life through the senses of your animal. Opening to all that's going on around you, experience the world through your animal's awareness. [5 minutes.]

8. When you are ready, say goodbye and release the connection with your spirit animal. Take one deep breath and then breathe naturally to feel centered and grounded within your body. [1 minute.]

9. Open your eyes and record your experiences.

JOURNAL PROMPTS

*What was your experience?
How was it different from your normal perspective? Were you shocked to find that reality is relative, dependent upon sensory experiences?
Will shifts in awareness you felt alter the way you perceive waking life?*

INTEGRATING ANIMAL GUIDANCE IN EVERYDAY LIFE

When I first started having long conversations with animals, I'd wonder how I could ever remember all that we covered, not to mention the nuances of what we shared. While in that deep quiet space of interior communication, I didn't want to interrupt the flow to record my thoughts, but I didn't want to forget anything either.

It was the animals who reassured me—Don't worry; we'll be there. I soon discovered what they meant. Minutes, hours, or even days later as I took notes on our conversation, I would suddenly feel that animal's presence as if it were looking over my shoulder, adding things I had forgotten, clarifying, or commenting. This was tremendously helpful—not only for recalling the subtleties of our conversation, but also for allowing the animal to share its current point of view.

Animals may show up to help us remember details or offer additional insights and support.

INTEGRATION

Integrating animal guidance into everyday life is an exercise in creativity, flexibility, and openness. It can also be great fun. In the example above, I had a need both to remember the details of conversation and remain in the flow. The animals responded with a brilliant solution, one I may not have thought of or even imagined on my own.

Integration may require us to build bridges between worlds. We may need to stretch ourselves, to dance lightly in the space that accesses both creative and logical thought, to open our awareness in a way that both notices symbolic language and understands it clearly.

I think of integration as a process of coming home to self. Perhaps this is our natural state of being—open and aware. At ease in the natural flow of living, we can accept the help, suggestions, advice, and different perspectives of others, and incorporate what fits into our personal lives. By exploring a wide range of experiences and assimilating what we learn, we deepen and expand.

TIPS TO REMEMBER

BE CURIOUS AND CREATIVE—To cultivate integration, build a foundation of curiosity and creativity. You can take any of the ideas and exercises in this book and adapt them to fit your needs. Use the tools you have learned to open doorways and initiate conversations. Be inventive, adding your unique flair and style to basic techniques. The more inspired and original you are, the greater range of experiences you'll have—not to mention fun.

BE OPEN—Integration isn't something to plan in advance. Rather, be open to the opportunities that present themselves. At times it is better to be empty of ideas, so that we can fill ourselves with the possibilities that come to light. Take time to listen, observe, and explore. Stay alert to clues and follow with a spirit of wonder.

BE FLEXIBLE—Sometimes we need to think and sometimes we need to feel. Integration is a dance, a lively two-step that keeps us on our toes. Exercise agility of mind and sensitivity to feelings so that you can see clearly and act accordingly in a graceful and balanced way.

THE TEACHINGS OF TURTLE AND TIGER:
A Sample Guide to Integration

The following story illustrates some of the intriguing ways that spirit animals interact with us and some of the creative ways we may integrate their teachings into everyday life.

THE ROAD AHEAD

You move to a new town and are seeking a job. After going on several interviews, you receive two offers of employment.

That night, you have a dream: walking down a deserted street, you come to a T-intersection. On your right, a box turtle sits in the middle of the road. On your left, a miniature tiger paces up and down the street. You are uncertain which way to proceed.

On waking, you note the correlation between your dream and the job offers. Turtle and Tiger are appropriate representatives, for one job is a sedate, secure, and rather boxed-in position, while the other requires an active, slightly aggressive demeanor. Turtle or Tiger? The dream does not offer a hint as to which route to choose.

Weighing the pros and cons of both jobs, you find it difficult to make a decision. In meditation, you ask the Universe to send you a sign.

TURTLE'S ANSWER
That evening a friend invites you for dinner. While in the ladies' room, you find a silver bracelet. Its intricate design features seven turtles linked tip to tail. You give it to the maître d' and return to your friend. A few moments later, the waiter delivers it to a woman at a neighboring table. He points in your direction and the woman thanks you profusely for returning her bracelet.

You later realize that the event revealed an answer to your question. Though you did not think it at the time, returning the turtle bracelet to its rightful owner may reflect your deeper feelings that the sedate job represented by Turtle belongs to someone else. Perhaps it's not logical to connect a bracelet with a job, but the symbolism makes sense to you, and you feel excited, as if you've paid attention to a message that is speaking to a deeper part of your being.

ANOTHER DREAM
That night you dream you are in a jungle. A young tiger is stalking you. Though it is small, you sense its strength and power. You enter a clearing and sit upon a boulder. Slinking from the jungle, the tiger sits in front of you and places

Encountering a young animal may indicate early stages of guidance.

one paw upon your knee. No longer frightened, you reach out and touch the tiger on its nose.

On waking, you again feel very excited to perceive the deeper meanings beneath appearances. Your action of returning the turtle bracelet indicated the slow-paced job was not for you. You are on another path now, for the actions of your dream lead you out of the jungle to a clearing—an opening—and the job represented by Tiger.

As you record your dream, you notice other clues, such as where you placed your finger: on tiger's nose. Is that a pun, foretelling that you will touch what Tiger knows?

APPRENTICE TO TIGER

After accepting the job, you enthusiastically make a list of Tiger's teachings and abilities: to prowl silently, to see clearly, to spring into action when the time is right. You read about tigers, though it is not so much facts you are after as deep wisdom. As an apprentice to Tiger's skills and energies, you want to know what Tiger knows.

After several months on the job, you are asked to make a presentation. For the first time, you become nervous and wonder if you have what it takes to succeed. Sitting at home, feeling despondent, you glance at the altar you made to Tiger soon after landing the job. It features a photograph of Tiger, a candle (to see in the dark), and several small mirrors (to reflect Tiger's presence within yourself). Lighting the candle, you request Tiger's help.

Light and reflection are two powerful ways of invoking energy and presence.

A stalking tiger teaches confidence, composure, and inner strength.

Opening to guidance, you turn on a documentary about tigers and ask Spirit of Tiger to please show you what you need to see. You find yourself drawn to the way tigers move. Whether stalking or exploring, they are so graceful and self-possessed. Yes—that is what you need!

You practice walking like Tiger— purposefully, confidently. Every day, you remind yourself to be like Tiger, silently commanding the respect of those around you. It's a subtle yet potent shift, not only of movement but of being, and the more you do it the more resolute you become.

THE FINAL TEST

Well prepared for your presentation, you enter the room like a tigress, serious and self-assured. You speak in a similar manner—clear and focused. All is going well until an older man interrupts you with a question. As he rambles, you sense the energy in the room dissipating, your authority waning.

Be creative when incorporating your spirit animal's skills into daily life.

Sensing disrespect as the man continues to prattle, you tap your nails upon the table. You have grown them longer and shaped them sharper than usual, a bit like a tiger, though the dark red polish was your idea. The clicking of nails is not loud, but jarring enough to create a short pause, which you utilize to thank the gentleman for his comments, sum up his question, and answer in a way that reveals both your knowledge and no-nonsense approach.

The presentation is a great success and soon after you are promoted. In only a few short months—with Tiger's help—your life has changed dramatically.

GIVING BACK

A few months later, on holiday in India, you visit a sanctuary that cares for injured tigers, with the aim of returning them to the wild. You are impressed with the staff's dedication and offer a generous donation. It feels right to give back for all that Tiger has given you. As you leave the sanctuary, a volunteer presses a small, hand-carved, gold-leafed tiger into your hands as thanks.

Back home, you place the statue on your desk. It reminds you of Tiger's many lessons: to pay attention; to assert yourself with confidence; to be firm yet fair. Guardian, protector, and mentor, Tiger's spirit shines through the little statue, a golden tribute to your mutual respect and evolving friendship.

Gifts featuring an animal teacher may indicate your progress.

DISCUSSION

By accepting invitations from spirit animals and following their teachings, we may begin to integrate their knowledge and skills into our lives. Not easily planned in advance, integration is a step-by-step process of noticing clues, discerning deeper meanings, and incorporating the helpful suggestions, ideas, and hints of wisdom into our daily experiences. A few examples using the sample story on the previous pages:

LINK DREAM MESSAGES TO WAKING LIFE—Turtle and Tiger offer two different paths. Neither one is more right than the other; rather, they represent a choice. The box turtle in the dream symbolizes a job that is "boxed in," safe, and secure. The pacing tiger points to a position involving movement, acuity, and perhaps a challenge.

CONTEMPLATE DEEPER MEANINGS—After asking the Universe for a sign, you find a silver turtle bracelet that you return to its rightful owner. On reflection, you perceive the deeper symbolism and understand that following Turtle is not your path.

CONSIDER THE DETAILS—In a second dream, Tiger first stalks and then approaches you in a clearing (reflecting your movement from fear to clarity of thought?). Note the specifics: Tiger places its paw upon your knee (in answer to your needs?) and you touch Tiger on the nose, suggesting precision—a foreshadowing of what Tiger already knows.

NOTE PATTERNS—It's interesting that Tiger initially appears in miniature, then young and small. While its diminutive first appearance only hints at possibility, Tiger grows in size as you embrace its energy more fully.

Sometimes *not* following an animal's path is part of our teaching.

ENGAGE ENTHUSIASM—You study Tiger's teachings and skills, and honor Tiger with an altar. Your actions reveal a desire to learn more and reflect your commitment to the process.

ASK FOR HELP AND ACCEPT GUIDANCE—When discouraged, you appeal to Tiger for help and are guided to see what you need to know. Mimicking Tiger's movements helps you access your own inner strength. Moving like Tiger allows you to draw energy from your spirit animal and eventually manifest Tiger's spirit within yourself.

ADAPT CREATIVELY—The way you grew and shaped your nails, reminiscent of tiger claws, is subtle yet powerful. Tiger's power is activated with a simple tapping of those nail-claws, allowing you to regain your authority. Tiger helps you present the strongest you that you can be.

RESPECT AND GIVE BACK—Months later you feel called to help tigers that need aid. By giving back, you honor the natural give-and-take of exchange, proving a friend and supporter to Tiger. In turn, you are given a golden tiger carving, a token suggesting accomplishment and permanence. Anchoring a corner of your desk, Tiger represents your rise to success and offers you future assistance.

When opportunity presents itself, consider giving back to the animals who have helped you.

YOU CAN DO IT TOO

Integrating animal wisdom into our lives need not be difficult. Pay attention; embrace opportunity. As you welcome and follow the teachings that so many animals offer freely, you may find your life shifting from the ordinary to the extraordinary.

CONCLUSION

In the wild or in our homes, present as spirit guides, messengers, companions, or mentors, animals bring us so very much. In addition to their unique lessons, animals urge us to be present and bring our best, most aware self to life.

Every time we meet an animal, we are offered the gift of relationship. How that relationship evolves depends at least partly on what we bring to the table. At a certain point, we might ask: what can I do for you?

Sometimes the answer is simply to remember an animal's words of advice or act upon its suggestions. Sometimes we are nudged to learn more about a particular species, maybe a species the world is not fond of—snakes, alligators, mosquitos—and help educate others. And sometimes we are asked to share what we have learned about our experiences and ourselves with the world at large.

PASS IT ON

One of my favorite places is a small lake high in the mountains. One summer while hiking around the lake, I came upon a stone shrine. It wasn't simply a pile of stones, but rather an artistic arrangement of different-sized rocks— jutting here, balancing there—forming a sculpture that must have taken hours to construct.

Trust yourself.
Encourage others.
Inspire beauty.
Embrace joy.
Love with wild abandon.

I noticed it was situated not far from the hole of a marmot. Perhaps the sculptor created the work as a tribute to Marmot, or as a reminder to notice the small things in life. Or perhaps the artist simply desired to arrange natural objects in a way that would inspire others. My heart smiled at this message of encouragement from an anonymous stranger.

CHANGE YOURSELF, CHANGE THE WORLD

One of the most powerful ways to give back to animals is to share our experiences with other humans, helping to awaken global awareness of our deeper connection with all life. Sometimes people need to hear of the "strange encounters" we have had with animals or animal spirits in order to believe that their experiences are real and meaningful too.

Maybe you write a book about what you know of animal spirits. Maybe you create art that arouses compassion or prompts awakening. Maybe simply by telling your stories to friends and family, you help them to better understand that all living beings deserve respect and love.

By sharing our views, we may excite others and influence their future actions. By motivating others to share their animal stories, we become instigators of awareness. Together, we help to raise the collective consciousness of all.

CELEBRATE!

The more we connect in heartfelt ways— with each other, with ourselves, and with other species—the greater our participation, enjoyment, and celebration of the big party called life.

Become an ambassador of awareness by sharing what you've learned. In doing so, you may inspire others to deepen in appreciation of animals, nature, self, and spirit. Trust the journey of all you've experienced and honor the ways you've changed. Remember: by changing ourselves, we also change the world.

GLOSSARY

ANIMAL ALTAR
A sacred space (often a small table or shelf) that features an arrangement of figurines, photographs, carvings, fur, feathers, and/or other meaningful animal representations. Animal altars can help us to remember, honor, and invoke the teachings of a specific animal or group of animals in daily life.

ANIMAL COMMUNICATION
Connecting heart-to-heart and mind-to-mind with an animal so that we may share feelings, thoughts, ideas, and experiences.

ANIMAL GUIDE
A living animal or animal spirit that guides us, often offering support, clarification, advice, wisdom, and/or illumination. Animal guides generally work with us in ongoing ways over a long period of time.

ANIMAL MESSENGER
An animal that appears at a crucial moment or key juncture to remind us of something, point us in a particular direction, or encourage us in a specific way. Animal messengers generally appear for a short period of time, deliver their message, and then leave.

DREAM WORLD
Our personal dreamscape as well as the shared dreaming environment that allows connection with other beings. Animal guides often make use of the dream world to initiate first contact and open us to their teachings.

EARTH ENERGY
The energy of the Earth as a living being. Often felt as an energetic emanation or humming vibration, Earth energy speaks to us in different ways.

FETISH
A small representation of an animal—usually carved stone, wood, or bone—that carries its teaching and may be imbued with its spirit. Holding or carrying a fetish can help us to access that animal's skills and wisdom.

GROUNDING
Connecting to the Earth as well as our foundational self. Grounding helps link inner-world experiences with our conscious self so that we may use the wisdom garnered in practical ways.

INNER WORLD
The vast inner expanse of our psyche and subconscious. Inner-world journeys take place in interior landscapes, which are not necessarily subject to the same rules of reality as the outer world.

INTEGRATION

To combine and bring our experiences, insights, thoughts, and feelings together so that we may understand in larger, more holistic ways. As the roots of this word imply, integration is to "make whole."

JOURNEYING

A deepening of consciousness that allows for inner-world travel and adventure. Journeying is a way of communicating with our spirit self as well as with spirit animal guides and teachers.

LUCID DREAMING

To be consciously aware that one is dreaming within a dream. Lucid dreaming allows us to explore the dream world with the conscious knowledge that we are asleep and dreaming.

MEDITATION

Entering a deepened state of consciousness that allows us to relax, clear the mind, focus awareness, contemplate, or explore interior worlds. There are many forms of meditation with different aims. In this book meditation is used as a launching pad for inner-world exploration.

ORACLE/ORACLE CARDS

Oracles are messages, traditionally believed to be connected with divine guidance. Animal oracle cards present images of various animal guides. When drawn intuitively, such cards can help us identify and connect with the type of animal guidance we need.

POWER ANIMAL

An animal that lends its skills, perceptions, and expertise to our daily lives. Power animals are generally spirit-based, though we may perceive their presence through a living animal. In this book, the terms power animal, spirit animal, and animal guide are used somewhat interchangeably.

PROJECTION

This word comes from the Latin meaning "throw forth." Projections are disowned energies that we throw forth (or project) onto other people or situations so as not to have to confront them within ourselves. It's wise to be aware of one's projections.

SHADOW ANIMAL

Animals that reveal key issues or teachings that our conscious self would like to forget. Shadow animals are typically those we fear, though they offer great wisdom to those who are willing to perceive beyond the surface projection. With the help of shadow animals, we may reconnect with the lost, forgotten, and denied selves that live beneath our conscious awareness.

SHAMANISM

An ancient spiritual practice rooted in the experiential knowledge that we are all integral parts of nature. Shamanism is a healing practice, a path to inner wisdom, and a means to find deepened connection with all life.

SHAMANIC BREATHING

In this book, shamanic breathing is a technique that focuses on centering awareness by connecting with Earth and Sky energies as a means to both deepen and expand consciousness.

SKY ENERGY

Energy represented by the Sky. For some, Sky energy relates to the heavens or the divine; for others, Sky energy represents a spiritual connection or connection with the higher (crown and above) chakras.

SOFT EYES

A soft, dreamy, intuitive way to perceive energy. By relaxing your eyes and allowing your vision to slightly blur or "soften" you may begin to sense beneath superficial appearances and perceive the deeper essence of life.

SPIRIT ANIMAL

Usually existing in spirit form, though sometimes manifesting through living animals, spirit animals work with us in a wide variety of ways. Spirit animals generally focus their teaching on our spiritual development, and we often develop a personal relationship with them as guardians, guides, and mentors.

SYNCHRONICITY

A term coined by Carl Jung denoting two events that occur simultaneously and seem to be related in a significant way though there is no perceptible causal connection.

TELEPATHY

Literally "feelings at a distance," telepathy allows us to connect energetically with others to share thoughts and feelings.

TOTEM ANIMAL

Traditionally an animal of significant spiritual meaning to a tribe or clan, totem animals are often connected to ancient ancestral energies and provide ongoing support and guidance to a group of people through their species' teachings.

UNIVERSAL LANGUAGE

The timeless, shared language of all life, accessible to all beings.

FURTHER READING

Andrews, Ted.
Animal Speak.
Minnesota, US: Llewellyn, 1997.

Boone, J. Allen.
Kinship With All Life.
New York, US: HarperOne, 1976.

Brunke, Dawn.
Animal Voices, Animal Guides.
Vermont, US: Bear & Company, 2009.

Brunke, Dawn.
Animal Teachings.
London, UK: CICO Books, 2012.

Brunke, Dawn.
Dreaming With Polar Bears.
Vermont, US: Bear & Company, 2014.

Roads, Michael.
Journey into Nature.
California, US: HJ Kramer Inc, 1990.

Smith, Penelope.
Animal Talk.
Oregon, US: Beyond Words, 2008.

USEFUL WEBSITES

Animal Voices
www.animalvoices.net

The Foundation for Shamanic Studies
www.shamanism.org

International Association for the Study of Dreams
www.asdreams.org

Working With Animal Spirits
www.animalspirits.com

INDEX

CREDITS